MY FAMILY AT CHRISTMAS, 1970.
We're celebrating at my Aunt Mattie and Uncle Art's house in my hometown of Ontario, CA. That fake white-flocked tree with gold ornaments appeared annually for more than two decades. I never realized how well it went with the curtains and hanging lamp. My big bruiser brother, Mike, is four years my senior. My stay-at-home mom, Donna, is holding a terrarium wrapped in tissue. Compton High School class of 1958 voted her the Outstanding Homemaking student. She spoiled us rotten by cooking nearly everything from scratch, sewing clothes, and making sure we went to Disneyland and Knott's regularly. My workaholic used-car-dealer dad, Gary, is wearing his trademark Pendleton jacket and smile. That's me in front with asymmetrical bangs. I have no idea what happened to the teddy bear, but I'll never forget when the brown corduroy coat from Sears that I'm wearing got sucked out of the window of our 1971 Oldsmobile Cutlass. I shouldn't have held it up to the open window while we were speeding past the limit. Thankfully, I wasn't wearing it!

Holiday Jubilee

Charles Phoenix

with KATHY KIKKERT

Holiday Jubilee

CLASSIC & KITSCHY FESTIVITIES and FUN PARTY RECIPES

PROSPECT
·PARK·
BOOKS

CHARLES PHOENIX TEST KITCHEN

Five Four Three Two One * 16

Will You Be Mine? * 28

Hoppin' Down the Bunny Trail! * 40

Snap Crackle Pop * 56

Contents

New Year's resolutions, exchanging Valentines, dyeing eggs, fireworks, carving pumpkins, roasting turkeys, decorating the tree, and seeing Santa—these are time-honored traditions Americans have devoured for generations. We've wrapped our arms and hearts around the holidays and never let go. Once a year we circle back and do it all again.

Holidays are the most famous days of the year—iconic calendar superstars and unstoppable forces of nature. We can count on them. We look forward to them. They are there for us. It's unimaginable to think of life without them. Each comes complete with its own exclusive protocol, style guide, design, décor, stories, songs, menu, mojo, flavors, festivities, colors, and cast of characters.

We didn't invent the holidays in the 20th century, but that's when we perfected them. Clever, forward-thinking, modern merchants and manufacturers morphed fascinating folklore, relics of religion, and monumental milestones into foolproof pillars of pop-consumerism culture, economic superpowers, and round-the-calendar carousels of commerce moving mountains of merchandise. Mega malls, big-box retailers, and supermarkets couldn't survive without our spirited seasonal shopping sprees.

Holidays are a primal force of pop culture—the fruit filling of American pie, with whipped cream on top. There's no better excuse to stuff ourselves silly with all-you-can-eat pies, cakes, cookies, and, most of all, candy. Not only is sugar expected, it is required. Confectioners and chocolatiers thrive on Valentine's Day, Easter, Halloween, and Christmas. What would they be without their Sweethearts, Peeps, and candy corn and canes?

Holidays are demanding, calling on many of our skill sets: socializing, shopping, cooking, crafting, decorating, and dressing up. They have high expectations of us, and we of them. They are the ultimate invitation to give, get, party, sing, dance, prance, eat, drink, and be happy, happy, happy!

Other than happy birthdays, holidays are the happiest days of the year. Happy New Year, Happy Valentine's Day, Happy Easter, Happy Fourth of July. Even Halloween is happy, Thanksgiving is happy too, and Christmas is so happy, it gets its own exclusive word for happy: MERRY.

I love great traditions, but I also like moving them forward and inventing new ones. That's exactly what this book is all about. It's a big, fat, rollicking funfest tribute to holiday traditions past, present, and future. Let this mix-and-mingle buffet feast of my over-the-top, original Test Kitchen recipes and vintage images from my Kodachrome slide collection inspire your imagination and make your spirit soar! You're invited to celebrate the holidays like never before!

HOLIDAYS ARE SO RETRO!

"How nice that someone hung up billboards
announcing the time of the year...
in case someone in the family just can't
remember anymore..."

"And how much do we all seriously love
aluminum Christmas trees?
I KNOW!"

the RETRO HOLIDAY

HOLIDAYS AND KODACHROME FILM are a picture-perfect match made in pop culture heaven. They were born for each other. Holidays are the epitome of a Kodak moment, and vintage slides are at their best when they inspire ideas that blossom into new traditions.

Kodachrome slide film was a midcentury-modern miracle. I've been collecting and curating vintage Kodachrome slides since 1992, when I discovered an old blue shoebox of them in a dusty, musty thrift shop in Pasadena, CA. My life hasn't been the same since. In 1998, I began sharing my favorite "found photos" with audiences, and my slide-showbiz career began. I've been performing retro slide shows ever since. In the early 2000s, a couple of years into my on-and-off run of shows at the Egyptian Theater in Hollywood, December rolled around. That was my cue to dip into my collection and create a holiday show.

"This is Bob Hope's brother and Bette Davis's sister... both enjoying a Christmas Eve cigarette..."

"What do you give an 85-year-old for Christmas anyway? They have everything!"

JUBILEE SLIDE SHOW

It never occurred to me to do a show just about Christmas, even though it's by far the most photographed holiday. New Year's, Valentine's Day, Easter, the Fourth of July, Halloween, and Thanksgiving also had to be celebrated. Eventually, the shows expanded beyond vintage slides when I began including my Test Kitchen creations as part of the act.

No two performances are ever the same—I'm always discovering new material. I'm thankful that my retro holiday show has become an annual tradition for many friends, fans, and families. I can't imagine celebrating the season—all the seasons!—without them.

Collecting vintage Kodachrome slides is the most convenient way to time travel, my favorite kind of treasure hunt, and it's always a pleasure and a privilege to share my discoveries with you.

WELCOME TO MY TEST KITCHEN, the fun food lab where I craft and cook up eye-popping, edible party centerpieces and potluck pleasers made with classic American brand-name products. These are original recipes that reflect the retro sensibility I was born to celebrate! I'm talking about Sara Lee Pies stuffed in Betty Crocker Cakes, Velveeta Snowmen that melt into delicious dip, and Christmas lights molded in Jell-O. Butter-fried Froot Loops and Trix become New Year's confetti. I sculpt meatloaf mix into Valentine's hearts, Easter lambs, and scary Halloween rats, and I bring watermelons to life with fruity faces for the Fourth of July. You can even eat Oscar Mayer cocktail weenies right off the Christmas tree. Nothing is off-limits, there are no rules, and creativity is king. This is fun food, not fine food!

CHARLES PHOENIX TEST KITCHEN

The Test Kitchen began by chance

the moment I saw this foil-wrapped cone studded with multicolored-toothpick-skewered fruits, veggies, and cocktail weenies. Even the poodle likes it! I knew immediately that this space-age spectacular was edible Christmas centerpiece perfection. It was begging to be reincarnated for a new generation to enjoy, and I was the right man for the job. I christened it the ASTRO-WEENIE CHRISTMAS TREE (see page 154). The success of this seasonal spectacle inspired me to get back into the kitchen and wonder what other Enchanted Edible Centerpieces and Potluck Party Pleasers I could concoct.

"Puttin' the Kitsch in Kitchen!"

I aspire to be creative in every aspect of my life, to find the humor in just about everything, and to make up my own rules as I go. I've always enjoyed cooking and crafting but have never been hard-wired to follow instructions or recipes. In my kitchen, it's all about experimenting and taking chances. Everything I cook and craft is a test. I have no idea how it's going to turn out. That's why I call it the Test Kitchen.

Supermarket Superstars

My Test Kitchen is also a pop culture kitchen. Dreaming up new ways to put famous mass-produced, highly processed foods through the paces of yet another process inspires me, and giving the foods I grew up eating another life is my way of paying tribute to them. Plus, I like to know what their backstory is—when they were first introduced and where they came from.

Twist & Swag

Why, collectively as a society, have we turned our backs on crepe paper? Those classic rolls of colorful, crinkly, pulpy paper are party-décor-on-a-budget perfection. Decorating with crepe paper is both easy to do and easy on the pocketbook. Anyone can do it. There are no rules—except more is definitely more! Get a chair to stand on and some Scotch tape and start twisting and swagging until you just can't twist and swag anymore. Happy crepe papering!

1957 Party Chef by Cory

When I first saw this space-age electric skillet land in my kitchen, I thought it was a flying saucer.

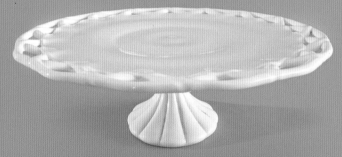

The Cake Plate

Every cake I've ever made has been served on this vintage milk glass cake plate. It's a family heirloom. My parents received it as a wedding gift in 1958.

No Fear of Food Coloring

I always say, "Have no fear of color." That goes for every part of my colorful life, including the Test Kitchen. Food coloring is something I've always enjoyed using as much and as often as possible. Since I

was a wee tot, I've marveled at that colorful quartet of teardrop-shaped, petite-plastic squeeze bottles. When I was about four, it occurred to me that the forest green tweed upholstery on our early American–style sofa wasn't quite bright enough. I went into the kitchen, found the food coloring, and promptly squeezed every drop of red, yellow, green, and blue on the sofa cushions. I don't remember the spanking I'm sure I got, but I do remember my mother saying, "Good thing these cushions are reversible, because if they weren't, you'd be dead."

Get Busy

Not only do I invite you to make my Test Kitchen creations, I dare you! I'll bet yours will turn out better than mine. Give it your personal touch. This is inspirational, not aspirational, cooking. Anyone can do this. Each dish is family friendly, fun to make, and a joyful experience, even if it does take over your life. Turn the prep into a pre-party event—enlist friends and family to help.

Showtime!

After all the time, energy, and expense you put into crafting your Test Kitchen concoction, presenting it is the most important moment in its life—and a significant moment in yours, too. The reveal of your incredible edible centerpiece is a happening, the pinnacle peak of your party. Savor the moment and milk it; this is what your guests came for. If there is alcohol involved, this is the time to propose a toast and say a spirited *Cheers!* Serve it up with glee, gusto, and a great big helping of American pride.

Be forewarned, however. Proceed at your own risk and always remember: If your special creation flops, fails, falls, collapses, and/or hemorrhages, act like it was supposed to happen that way. Your Test Kitchen creations need not be perfect. That's not what they're about. They're about humor, heart and soul, and having fun, fun, fun!

CHARLES PHOENIX TEST KITCHEN

13

DISNEYLAND 1964. Nothing says "Happy Holidays" like big boxes with human legs marching on Main Street, USA, at the "Happiest Place on Earth."

Five Four Three Two One!

WIND THE CLOCK, PUT ON YOUR PARTY HATS, CUE THE CONFETTI, AND POP THE CORK – it's New Year's, the most important, and impressive, ticktock of the calendar year. In the hours leading up to the minutes before the midnight moment, we get our glitz and glam on and prepare to make some noise. It's out with the old and in with the New Year's resolutions. Party Hearty. Go ahead, get a little loopy to take the leap, and when it's high time to say "Cheers," hold that glittering glass, brimming with bubbly, high and wide with pride. This is the moment you showed up for. 5-4-3-2-1...

HAPPY NEW YEAR !!!

KISS ME!

BOOZE & LEIS

NOISEMAKERS

"MR. NEW YEAR'S EVE"
No New Year's Eve play-list is complete without "Auld Lang Syne." For that we can thank GUY LOMBARDO. He famously performed the ages-old Scottish song recalling "times gone by" live on the radio, then later on TV, every New Year's Eve between 1929 and 1977, earning him the well-deserved nickname "Mr. New Year's Eve."

NEW YEAR'S EVE with GUY LOMBARDO and His Royal Canadians

DECCA RECORDS

DEAD MAN DANCING

19

FRIED CONFETTI,

the latest "I-can't-stop-eating-this" finger food, is a sweet and salty party snack sensation of the absolute highest order. Tots, kids, teens, adults, and senior citizens love this colorful mix of classic breakfast cereals tossed and toasted in melted salted butter! Eat it like popcorn, but be forewarned: Fried Confetti is ADDICTIVE!

GET THIS

1 ½ sticks salted butter
1 cup each:
Apple Jacks
Cap'n Crunch
Froot Loops
Trix
Honeycombs
Corn Pops
Lucky Charms

FRIED CEREAL SLUMBER PARTY!
Turn your New Year's Eve party into a sleepover. Invite your friends and relations to show up with a box of their favorite cereal!

WHAT'S YOUR MIX?
Personalize your Fried Confetti by mixing together a total of seven cups of your favorite puffed cereals. (Flake cereals do NOT work.) Name the mix after yourself! If your name is Tiffany, call it "Tiffany Mix"; for Melvin, it's "Melvin Mix!"

GET BUSY

Separate Marbits from Lucky Charms. Sift cereal to remove unwanted crumbs and dust. On LOW heat melt butter on stove top or electric skillet. When butter is melted, add cereal mixture. Toss continuously for 3 to 4 minutes until the room begins to smell of sweet buttered toasted cereal deliciousness. Make as much Fried Confetti at one time as your skillet can hold. For large party-sized bowls, fry each of your cereals separately, then mix. Remove from heat before cereal begins to brown. Don't stop stirring or it will burn! Try to control yourself from eating it all.

SHOWTIME

Pour while still warm into the biggest, most beautiful bowl you have. Sprinkle Marbits on top and serve with pride and joy. Then start making more because your guests have already gobbled it up!

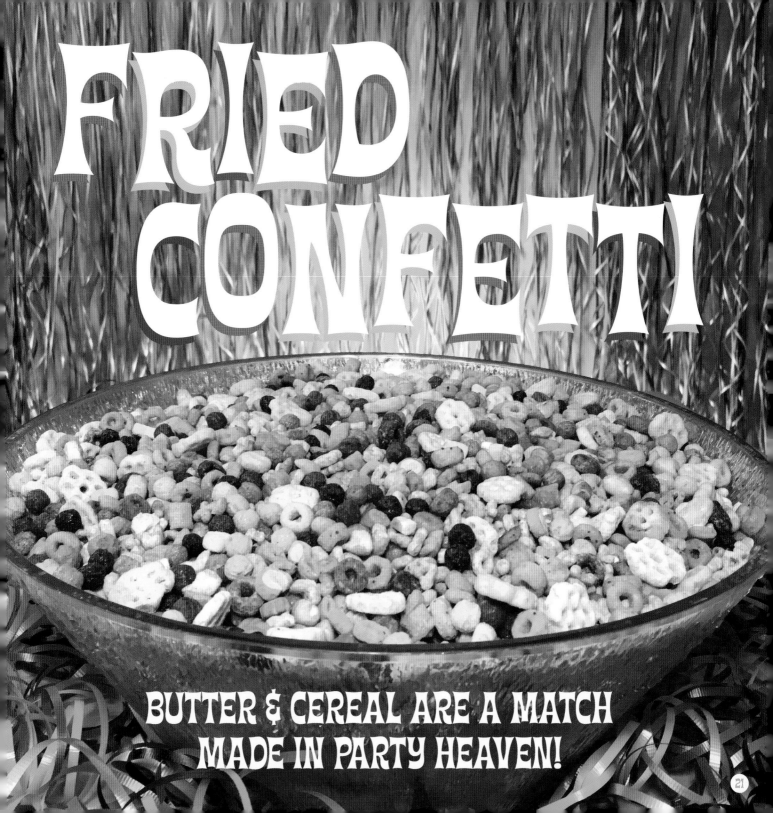

FRIED CONFETTI

BUTTER & CEREAL ARE A MATCH MADE IN PARTY HEAVEN!

Flower Power

THE ROSE PARADE, a colorful cavalcade of rolling flower sculptures, prized show horses, and champion marching bands, has been a New Year's Day tradition in Pasadena, CA, since 1890.

Rose Queen and Her Court

We don't have a king in Southern California, but we have a queen: the Rose Queen. Her reign is brief, just one year. She works her way up through the charm schools and debutante balls of the San Gabriel Valley, and her first call of duty is waving properly to her subjects while strapped to a flower-festooned barge and cradling a super-sized bouquet of red roses like a baby.

BEST & WORST OF SHOW

THE FROST THAT KILLS THE PUMPKIN, sponsored by the city of Van Nuys in 1957, has got to be the ugliest Rose Parade float ever. Gerber daisies have never looked so bad! But every dark cloud has a silver lining. As fate would have it, the very next year Van Nuys gave us the greatest float of all time: WHATTA DREAM, a giant piece of cherry pie. Just look at the way the early-morning sun captures the golden, buttery, perfectly pinched crust, and the way that giant breast of French vanilla ice cream melts so deliciously between those plump, juicy cherries. This flavorful floral fantasy is Rose Parade perfection.

Wake Up and Smell the Roses

The Rose Parade is far more dazzling and fragrant in person than on TV. The delightful detail and spectacle of it all is thrilling to see up close. I attend every year I'm in town. I arrive just before sunup to get a "back-stage" sneak peek of the floats, marching bands, and queen and her court taking their places. My favorite spot to watch the parade is where it officially begins. To me there is no better way to start the new year!

MY FAVORITE MARTIAN!

BLAST-OFF!

FLY ME TO THE MOON!

TORRANCE

QUEEN OF OUTER SPACE

TLE ROCK

TAKE ME TO YOUR LEADER!

The Race for Roses

The Rose Parade breaks the sound barrier and blasts off to outer space with jets, rockets, astronauts, and aliens!

The War of the Roses

OUR FIRST QUARREL

The furniture is knocked over, the lamp has toppled, the fern has fallen, the pictures on the wall are crooked, and the bookshelves are a mess. This looks like more than a quarrel to me. I'm glad they've made up, but the place is trashed! I want to know who at the California Exchange Club thought that a domestic-violence-themed float would be appropriate for the 1959 Rose Parade. Can you imagine "Our First Quarrel" as the theme of a float today–or better yet, theme of the entire parade?

Riding on Roses

I ALWAYS DREAMED of riding on a Rose Parade float, and much to my shocking surprise, my dream came true. The gracious ticket to ride in the 123rd Annual Rose Parade on the "Enchanted Paradise" float came from the Downey Rose Float Association. Waving with gusto and smiling wide beside a fire-spewing volcano, two tropical waterfalls, a trio of tiki gods, and five teenage beauty queens along the three-mile parade route was surreal, to say the least. By the time it was over, my arms were weak and my rosy cheeks were twitchy. Be careful what you wish for in life—your dreams may come true!

Will You Be Mine?

ORDER THE ROSES, CUE CUPID, CALL THE QUEEN OF HEARTS, AND PUCKER UP— it's Valentine's Day, the loveliest, lustiest, most romantic day of the year. We woo our sweethearts in various ways in hopes that a winged, curly-headed toddler will draw back his bow and shoot us in the heart. For adults, Valentine's Day is a night move. It's roses for romance and candy for kisses. If you're lucky, you'll get more than a beautiful bouquet of roses or a heart-shaped box of candy! But first, at least be polite and ask, "Will You Be Mine?"

For Her · Everybody loves WOOLWORTH'S VALENTINE'S DAY Feb. 14th · For Him

Grade-School Sweethearts
Valentine's Day craft project class portrait, Wilmington, CA, 1955.

My Funny

You LIGHT UP my life

On Valentine's Day, DEAR.

I'm just WILD about you VALENTINE

39-VC 749-3
MADE IN U.S.A.

America's love affair with Valentine's Day began in the 1850s when the first Valentine's Day card was mass-produced in Massachusetts. Hallmark began printing valentines in 1916, about the same time kids began trading cards in the classroom. By the 1950s, grade-schoolers celebrated the heart-shaped holiday by exchanging flirtatious cards printed with perky poems and silly, sassy sayings and illustrated with cute, cartoonish characters.

Sweet Talk

The seasonal-shaped sugar pellets that we lovingly call Sweethearts have been sending fun, flirtatious messages like "be mine," "too cute," "kiss me," and "call me" since 1901, when they were introduced by Necco, of Revere, MA.

Brach's Valentine Hearts

2½ OZ. NET WT.

Valentine

LET'S BE FRANK! I WANT YOU FOR MY VALENTINE!

59VK-74 7-20 MADE IN U.S.A.

You AUTO be my VALENTINE

NEPHEW

Just for You

Pink knotty-pine cabins and delightful directional signage at Bushkill Falls House Resort, where you could experience, as the brochure promised, "The Honeymoon of Your Heart's Desire."

Heart-Shaped Honeymoon

In the 1950s and '60s, the Poconos pitched itself as the "Honeymoon Capital of the World." On the west bank of the Delaware River in Pennsylvania, nestled in hills lush with lakes and waterfalls, were several oh-so-romantic resorts catering to newlyweds.

You Are ENTERING the *Land of Love*

LAND OF LOVE, LAKEVILLE, PA
You have arrived at the Cove Haven Resort, "Honeymoon Capital of the World," famous since 1958 for heart-shaped tubs and beds.

HEARTS & CRAFTS

RED HEARTS and yards of ruby-red tulle gathered, tied, and finished with paper doilies festively frame a doorway, or crepe-paper-covered Styrofoam hearts dotted with pink carnations and ferns fresh from the florist— two picture-perfect ideas for lovely Valentine's party pix.

Have a Heart

Valentine's Day definitely wins the prize for best candy box of the year. Nothing says I LOVE YOU like a giant, frilly, fancy cardboard heart full of bite-size chocolates filled with nuts, nougats, and crème centers. Each piece is an aphrodisiac. What's your favorite?

Valentine's Day's Other Main Course!

Every holiday deserves its own special meatloaf, and Valentine's Day is no exception. Inspired by classic tattoos and *I Love Lucy*, this dinner dish of deliciousness is sure to get you the dessert you really want! Savor the flavor of this ketchup-topped, twice-baked, tater-tot-stuffed meatloaf for two, served on a bed of buttered mashed potatoes and decorated with fresh veggies. It's the most romantic main dish to come along in years.

GET THIS

3 lbs. of your grandma's meatloaf recipe, mixed and ready to be baked

1 bag frozen tater tots

2 lbs. cooked mashed potatoes

2 small cans seasoned tomato paste

1 red, 1 green, and 1 yellow bell pepper

1 bag brussels sprouts, halved

1 basket grape tomatoes

8 carrots, peeled and quartered

1 crab apple

Large piping bag with large round tip

GET BUSY

Bake tater tots according to instructions. Shape meatloaf mix into heart. Cover with tater tots. Spread foil-covered baking sheet with 1 inch mashed potatoes and place meatloaf tater tot side down on potatoes. Spread with tomato paste on top. Pipe your message in mashed potatoes. Cut peppers into strips and decorate meatloaf with veggies like you mean it. Bake at 350° for 1 hour.

SHOWTIME

Keep your I LOVE YOU meatloaf in the oven on warm until it's time to serve your savory surprise. When it's time to eat, sit your Valentine down at the table and present your meat masterpiece with a passionate kiss, and then say, "And guess what's for dessert?" Enjoy!

I Love You

Meatloaf

CREAM-SOAKED

COOKIE CAKE

of Love ♥

OREOS, NUTTER BUTTERS, CHIPS AHOY, FUDGE STRIPES, AND CIRCUS ANIMALS

are each soaked separately in cream and baked in their own cake layer, which is stacked and slathered with milk chocolate frosting and more cookies! We all love dunking cookies in milk, but this is more like drowning them in cream. The creamy, dreamy cookie-and-cake combo is, of course, rich and moist, but in an unexpected, irresistible, cheerfully cheesecake kind of way.

GET BUSY

MIX CAKE BATTER according to box instructions in one large bowl.

SOAK COOKIES: Break up 1 bag each of cookies into smaller pieces. Evenly divide half-and-half into 5 cake pans. Fill pans with enough of the various broken cookie pieces (1 kind of cookie per pan) to absorb the half-and-half overnight. Fudge Stripes and Circus Animals will require some additional cookies from the second package to absorb all the half-and-half. Keep adding broken cookies until virtually all the half-and-half is absorbed and the consistency is somewhere between paste and goop. Remove cookie mush from pans, set aside, and wash pans.

BAKING COOKIES INTO CAKE: Spray clean cake pans with PAM. Line bottom of each pan with parchment paper. Flour sides. Pour ¾ inch of batter into each pan. Spoon 1 kind of the soaked cookies atop batter in each of the 5 pans. Cover cookie and cream mixture completely with another ¾ inch of batter. Bake cakes according to box instructions, but keep in mind additional baking time may be required. Use the classic toothpick test to make sure the cakes are cooked through.

Carefully remove from pans and cut off the domes with a serrated knife. Eat them while nobody is looking. Wrap each layer in plastic wrap and freeze until you're ready to stack and frost.

FROSTING AND FINISHING: Frost generously, refrigerate cake to firm it up, then decorate with Oreos, Nutter Butters, Chips Ahoy!, Fudge Stripes, and Circus Animals on the sides and top.

GET THIS

2 packages Oreos

2 packages Nutter Butters

2 packages Chips Ahoy!

2 packages Fudge Stripes

2 packages Circus Animals

½ gallon half-and-half (substitute heavy cream if you don't want to live)

4 boxes white cake mix

6 tubs milk chocolate frosting

5 9-inch cake pans

SHOWTIME

Gather your sweethearts around the cake. Just before you cut out an entire quarter of the cake, declare your eternal love for them and push that knife down through all five layers with karate-chop force and the wild roar of a lion. Reveal the intoxicating innards with unbridled pride and joy. Serve each piece with a hug, squeeze, and big kiss!

HOPPIN' DOWN the BUNNY TRAIL

BOIL THE WATER, POP OPEN THE PEEPS, AND STRAP ON YOUR BONNET– it's Easter, the most celebrated Sunday morning and eggcentric day of the year. We begin the birth of spring by dyeing. We have no interest in what's inside the "incredible edible" chicken treat–we're interested only in what's on the outside. Sunday at sunup, we suit up in our best deluxe-dapper dress, collect our colorful confection-filled Easter basket, and let the candy consuming begin. Biting the head off the chocolate bunny is a big, mouthful moment. The sweet stuff induces a sugar rush that fuels the morning's main event: the hunt. Whoever finds the most eggs wins the day. Before we swarm the dinner table, like bees to Honey Baked Ham, we eat more candy. And that's what's for dessert, too. But don't spike your blood sugar too high or you just might think you see Peter Cottontail hoppin' down the bunny trail!

EASTER BEAST

Clad only in an apron and clown collar, this big bad bunny looks like a squirrel and a horse had a baby.

OPEN EGG HOUSE

SANTA'S VILLAGE, LAKE ARROWHEAD, CA

The well-dressed half gentleman, half rabbit creature is the host with the most. He welcomes Little Bo Peep and her two sheep inside to see the baby bunnies. The architect who hatched this giant stucco egg house sure did an eggcellent job!

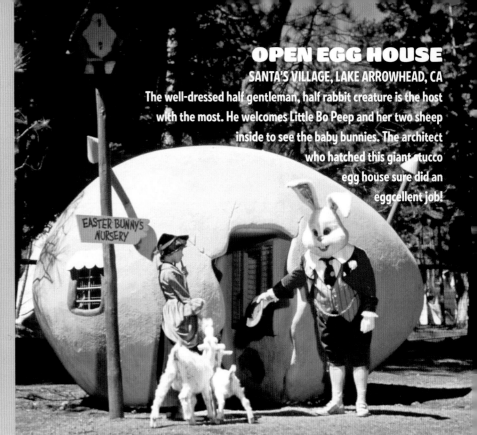

EASTER BUNNY'S NURSERY

Remember the Alamo Bunny

JOSKE'S DEPARTMENT STORE
San Antonio, TX, 1962

This big blow-up bunny spent the Easter season overlooking the Alamo. He was perched above the main entrance of Texas's oldest department store, founded in 1867.

BARRY AND BUNNY

Taking a break while shooting an episode of **STORAGE WARS** with Barry Weiss. Yes, we discovered the bunny suit in a storage locker, and yes, he made me put it on!

SANTA'S VILLAGE

JEFFERSON, NH, 1962

For all those times you wanted to strike a pose between the legs of a giant Easter bunny, Santa's Village has you covered. This big guy has been a picture-perfect poser prop since 1953.

HERE COMES PETER COTTON-TAIL

PETER COTTONTAIL is the rabbit who wants to be human. He certainly dresses like one, and a quite dapper one at that. His delightful attire sets the Easter Sunday style standard. Peter is the bearer of brightly colored baskets brimming with candy and a chocolate sculpture of himself. If we're lucky, we'll get to meet him at the mall for a proper Easter portrait. We'll be even luckier if we see him on Easter Sunday. He first made his presence known in 1910 as Peter Rabbit, when he hopped off the pages of a book by Thornton Burgess and into America's collective conscience. He's been the superstar of Egg Day ever since.

Hoppin' Hit Record

The classic Easter song "Here Comes Peter Cottontail" was a big hit in 1949, peaking on the Billboard chart at #8.

PAAS 29¢
EASTER EGG *Pure Food* COLOR KIT
COLD WATER *FIZZ* TABLETS
Give bright INSTANT-COLOR

Happy Easter

6 COLOR TABLETS • 1 EGG DIPPER • 1 EASTER TRANSFER SHEET
1 PUNCH OUT EASTER WAGON • 6 TWIRLY TOPS

TO DYE FOR

I'M DYEING!

To do the traditional Easterly duty of egg dyeing, most of us choose Paas to transform our rainbow-colored assortment of eggs to hide, hunt, and fill our plastic-grass-packed Easter baskets. We owe a big, colorful, Easter-eggy thanks to druggist William Townley, who invented Easter-egg dye tablets in his Newark, NJ, drug emporium in 1880. He branded his five-color dye kits Paas, which comes from the word Passen, the Pennsylvania Dutch name for Easter. What would America's eggiest holiday be without PAAS?

EGGSPIRATION

The eggs aren't really "dying"– they're just getting colorized. And who doesn't love the tradition of dyeing eggs? I dye both white and brown eggs. I don't discriminate. The brown eggs add a rich warmth to the colors that you simply don't get with white ones.

HUEVOS WANTER

No backyard hiding place is off-limits. Not even the BBQ. After the eggs have been hidden, found, rolled around the Easter basket, counted, and kvelled over, they're pretty much as good as rotten. Too bad, because Easter-egg-salad sandwiches would make a perfect addition to any bunny-day brunch buffet.

EGG TREE

I love it when people confuse the holidays—like whoever decorated a tree with Easter eggs as though it were Christmas. And while we're on the subject of mixing it up, I think holidays need more eves. Why are New Year's and Christmas the only holidays with eves? It's not fair. Two eves simply aren't enough! We're totally missing out on HallowEVE, ThanksEVEning, and my favorite, EVEster!

EGG HUNT

EASTER WOULDN'T BE EASTER WITHOUT CANDY AND PLENTY OF IT. But unlike Christmas, Valentine's, and Halloween, you don't have to work for it. Neither seduction nor trick or treating are involved, and it doesn't matter if you've been naughty or nice. The jelly beans, egg-shaped confections, and chocolate bunnies simply appear nestled on a bed of pretty pastel plastic grass in a big, beautiful, discreetly delivered multicolored basket.

SUGAR SUNDAY

THE SHAPE OF SUGAR

Sugar eggs are exactly that: sugar and egg whites. Molding and decorating hundreds of sweet, hollow huevos is an Easter tradition for the Watkins-Augustine family in Welsh, LA. What began four generations ago has evolved into the best handmade panoramic sugar egg business on the planet, SugarEggs.com. Each one is a work of art.

THE EASTER BUNNY appears on his big day in many shapes and sizes, but none more importantly than molded in chocolate. Countless confectioners created these cute cocoa creatures for decades before 1948, when R. M. Palmer of East Reading, PA, masterminded the first machine to mass-produce hollow chocolate rabbits. Today, the Palmer bunny business remains family owned, and that marvelous midcentury machine is still molding masses of hollow hippity-hoppers, more than any other candy company in the USA.

PEEPS DEETS

Easter's iconic sticky-sweet marshmallow chicks were originally piped by hand beginning more than 90 years ago in a Brooklyn, NY, candy store. In 1953, candy man Sam Born discovered the chicks and hatched the idea to mass-produce them in his candy factory in Lancaster, PA. He invented the automatic Peeps piper, and Peeps have been power-piped perfectly every Easter since.

ASTRO-WEENIE PEEPS TREE

THE PERFECT SWEET & SAVORY EASTER CENTERPIECE
Peeps and cocktail weenies stuck with multicolored toothpicks on a tinfoil-wrapped Styrofoam cone.

EASTER BASKET BONNET
Vintage mannequin window display at Nickel Diner, downtown Los Angeles.

peeps

BIG BASKET

THE WORLD'S LARGEST EASTER BASKET, the centerpiece of Lakeview Park in Lorain, OH, was the brainchild of a child, the son of the park's superintendent. The unveiling happened just in time for Easter 1941. But the locals weren't terribly impressed until the next year, when the newspaper reported that the Easter Bunny had filled the giant basket with a dozen 75-pound cement eggs, which promptly became the ultimate collectibles for the town pranksters.

BONNET BOMB

My head is spinning over this tornado of tissue paper swirlin' and whirlin' in ways I've never seen before. For those of you wanting to get in touch with your inner milliner, let this colorful and crafty Egg Day headpiece be an inspiration. You can make one, too. But don't forget the chin strap–this bonnet can fly!

GRANDMA & GRANDPA JR.

This bro & sis power duo don't do Easter baskets, they do Easter boxes. Not only that, they celebrate Easter dressed up like their grandparents. What an eggscellent idea! I think this should be a new Easter tradition.

BONNETS, BASKETS & BOW TIES

Easter Parade

BURBANK, CA, 1958

Easter is the best-dressed, most delightfully dapper Sunday of the year. Traditionally, everyone sports fresh, fine new fashions for spring's supreme day. Churchyard egg-hunt-ready kids pose with baskets in hand. Standing command is a power-mom duo, one wrapped in a wannabe-glamorous man-made mink stole. But the most famous fashion statement of the day is the almighty Easter bonnet. Every female in this photo has one perched on her head. They're required!

FOR THOSE OF YOU WHO HAVE BEEN TO ONE OF MY RETRO HOLIDAY JUBILEE SHOWS, CHANCES ARE YOU REMEMBER MARY-CHARLOTTE. Who could forget this magical mirror image of that strawberry blond hair, peaches-and-cream complexion, and cigarette dangling from those red painted lips? Cut roses and squeezed lemons add color to the otherwise very blue bathroom that she has cleverly turned into a make-shift bar. Well, after all, it's Easter Sunday, and cocktails will be served!

Mary-Charlotte

EASTER SUNDAY
Phoenix, AZ, 1952

THE TEQULUA SUNRISE

Cheers to Mary-Charlotte!

**Bless your Easter brunch by offering her cocktail...
2 parts tequila to 1 part Kahlúa with several squeezes of lemon.**

THE ROSES ARE IN BLOOM, the grass is green, and there's a sampler platter of chaise longues... take your pick. This lovely lady would probably be posing with her best friend, Mary-Charlotte. But Mary-Charlotte is a little busy right now, mixing up some cocktails. You've heard of the Easter Sunrise and the Tequila Sunrise. Add a bit of Kahlúa and you've got the Tequlua Sunrise. Serve it with a squeeze.

LATER THAT AFTERNOON, our bartender, Mary-Charlotte, is sitting up just fine, but her friend is sucking foam out of the lawn furniture.

PUNCHING BUNNY

Swift began hamming it up in Eastham, MA, in 1835.
There is simply no better way to advertise
Swift's Premium Ham than on the belly of
a blow-up punching-bag bunny.

How to do your guests a favor on Easter...

Martha Logan's clever Easter Egg favors are easy to do—see the directions below. They'll make your Swift's Premium Ham look so gay. You always do your guests another kind of favor, too, when you serve Swift's Premium. For it's *America's favorite* ham. Brown Sugar Cured as only Swift knows how . . . s-l-o-w-l-y smoked over fragrant hardwoods . . . till every bite is juicy, tender, *delicious!*

Swift's Premium Ham

SWIFT—TO SERVE YOUR FAMILY BETTER

EASTER IS THE HAMMIEST DINNER DAY OF THE YEAR.

Porky Pig is the perfect main course
after the big egg hunt. That big fat ham
fits right in with Easter's pastel color
scheme—it's pretty in pink!

BAA-BAA BUTTER LAMB

Chocolate bunnies aren't the only animal-shaped edibles on Easter. While exploring Buffalo, NY, I stumbled upon Malczewski's Butter Lamb stand at the Broadway Market. Locals line up for their famous little lambs every spring, just as they have for decades. I'd never seen a butter lamb before. Much to my disappointment, I was told that they're only available during the Easter season. It was October. I was out of luck. I asked if they had just one left over. I was promised they didn't. I asked again. Finally, when my ask turned into a beg, sure enough, out came this one. I just about melted! And yes, it looks just like a guinea pig. But have you tried making butter look like a lamb lately?

Malczewski's
Easter Butter Lamb

Hams &

52

AM I BLUE LAMB CAKE

Easter knows no fear of food coloring!

RUDOLPH THE RED-NOSED LAMB CAKE

Never mind the fact that this little lamb cake is channeling Santa's superstar reindeer. I'd like to know who the creative culinary genius is who was able to dye Easter eggs to look exactly like slightly over-deep-fried corn dog nuggets. Corn dog manufacturers, take note!

The chocolate bunny isn't Easter's only party-animal edible. The **LEGENDARY LITTLE LAMB** occasionally makes an appearance, too, usually in the form of a coconut cake on the delicious dessert table.

Lambs

EASTER MEATLOAF of LAMB

It's a Springtime Dinner Delight!

This sheep-shaped **EASTER SUNDAY MAIN COURSE** is the savory reinvention of the classic lamb cake. It's the perfect mighty-meaty centerpiece for that post-egg-hunt holiday dinner.

As long as I've been performing my Retro Holiday Slide Show, I've included vintage images of funny Easter lamb cakes. Year after year, I threatened to buy one of those classic two-piece aluminum lamb-cake molds and bake one myself. So I finally ordered one, and the next day a baby sheep shape arrived on my doorstep. But when it came time to actually use it, I was feeling a bit more savory than sweet, so I decided that my little lamb should be made of molded meat. Yes, ground lamb would've been more apropos, but I opted for some good ol' ground cow.

GET THIS

3 lbs. of your grandma's meatloaf recipe, mixed and ready to be baked

8 cups stiff mashed potatoes

1 bag frozen corn, thawed

1 bag frozen peas, thawed

6 carrots, peeled and quartered

Large piping bag with large star tip

Classic lamb cake mold

14-inch oval platter

22 plastic spoons

22 dyed eggs

GET BUSY

Fill each of the two sides of the lamb cake mold almost to the top with meatloaf mixture. Bake at 350˚ until a probing meat thermometer reads 170˚, about 1 hour. Remove from pan, drain off excess fat, and let cool. Fill star-tipped piping bag with mashed potatoes and set aside. "Glue" lamb front and back together with more of the mashed potatoes. Firmly place whole lamb loaf on a mound of the remaining mashed potatoes on platter. Now the fun part: giving him his coat of curly wool. Squirt the reserved mashed potatoes from the pastry bag to give him a full coat. Cover the potato mound with thawed peas and corn. Press carrots into mashed potatoes, alternating with dyed eggs on plastic spoons into mashed potato base to frame him with a holy halo-esque starburst. Finally, give your little lamb life with a face of pea eyes and a small carrot-chip nose/mouth combo.

SHOWTIME

Vigorously ring the Easter dinner bell, gather guests around the dining room table, and present your Easter Meatloaf of Lamb with unbridled spring pride. Let everyone post selfies with him, then slice, serve, and wish everyone, "Happy Easter…Meatloaf of Lamb!" Rejoice!

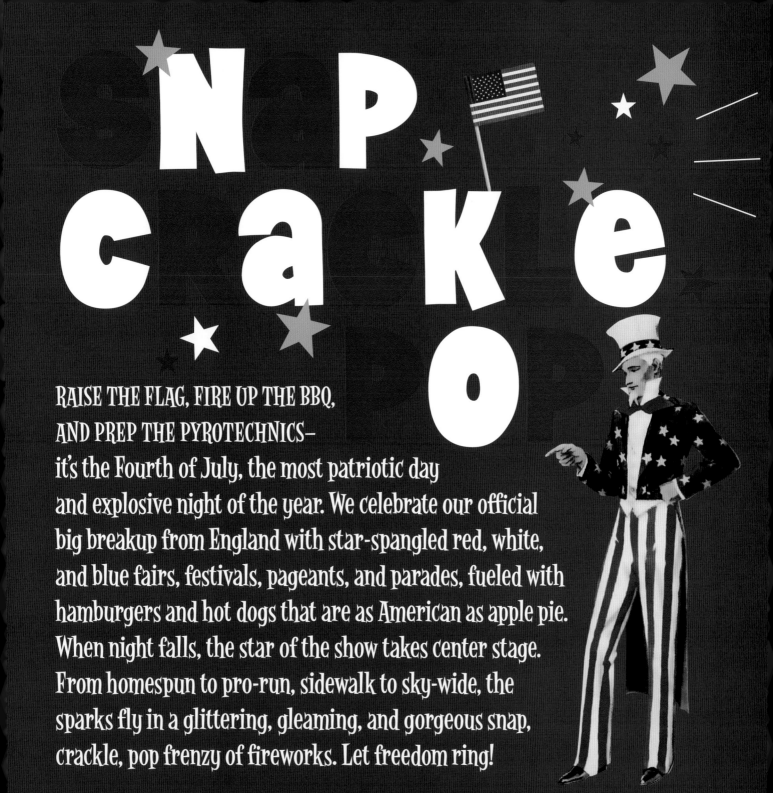

SNAP CRACKLE POP

RAISE THE FLAG, FIRE UP THE BBQ,
AND PREP THE PYROTECHNICS—
it's the Fourth of July, the most patriotic day
and explosive night of the year. We celebrate our official
big breakup from England with star-spangled red, white,
and blue fairs, festivals, pageants, and parades, fueled with
hamburgers and hot dogs that are as American as apple pie.
When night falls, the star of the show takes center stage.
From homespun to pro-run, sidewalk to sky-wide, the
sparks fly in a glittering, gleaming, and gorgeous snap,
crackle, pop frenzy of fireworks. Let freedom ring!

If you have something to say, spell it out in crepe paper on a parade float–like these proud-to-be-American siblings, ready to go and tow with their flag-flying, decorated-to-match tricycles.

BETSY ROSS by MARY BLAIR
A detail of a vacu-form plastic wall plaque for Johnson & Johnson by the legendary Disney artist.

Red, white, and blue meets midcentury mod at the most patriotic coffee shop I've ever had the pleasure of dining in. The Gettysburger and Yankee Doodle Ice Cream Sundae were the specialties of the house. Feel free to have a smoke, too–there are ashtrays on every table.

BETSY ROSS COFFEE SHOP, UPLAND, CA

SUPER RARE & THREADBARE

A classic little old lady proudly displays her homemade family heirloom, a 13-star centennial flag made for the Fourth of July in 1876.

Sparkling Sprinkler Portrait

This should be a fun family Fourth of July tradition: bathing suits, smiles, and water on high. Flags as a backdrop are required, sunglasses optional!

LONG MAY IT WAVE

HONK HONK, your Fourth of July ride is here! Meet the biggest, most luxurious, most powerful luxury car Ford Motor Company ever built: the all-new-for-1958 Mark III convertible by Continental. The most unusual feature of this space-age spellbinder is the reverse-slant power window that glides up and down with the flip of a switch. Too bad the horn didn't play "The Star-Spangled Banner."

CARS AND STRIPES FOREVER

NATHAN'S FAMOUS The nation's biggest hot dog-eating contest is an annual tradition on the Fourth of July at Nathan's on Coney Island, the most famous hot dog stand in the world. Local lore tells us the first competition happened on July 4, 1916, with four immigrant Americans settling a bet over who was the most patriotic. The record "Mustard Belt" winner ate 73 hot dogs in 11 minutes!

FRANKS ★ FOR THE FOURTH!

FROZEN FIREWORKS

Cherry, lime, and blue-raspberry-flavored Bomb Pops are my favorite frozen sweet treats. They're delicious every day, but I do limit them to just once a year, the Fourth of July. They first exploded into the supermarket freezer cases in 1956. Rocket Pops landed several years later.

MONSIEUR MUSTARD

French's isn't French at all, it's American, from Rochester, NY. Former flour miller George French introduced the hot dog's best friend at the 1904 St. Louis World's Fair.

WEENIE CRAFTS

Thank you forever and always to the almighty Hot Dog Association for these flavorful, festive, and fun Fourth of July crafts with weenies: weenie cannons, weenie rockets, and weenie firecrackers with celery strips for wicks.

EXCITING EDIBLE FOURTH OF JULY PARTY CENTER-PIECE

★

Foil-wrapped cabbage ball studded with veggies and cocktail weenies on long skewers finished with radishes stuck with frill picks.

ASTRO-WEENIE

APPETIZER EXPLOSION

UNCLE WATERMELON

The Fruit + Veggie-Faced Mascot that the Fourth of July Has Been Waiting For!

GOT THIS

The best-looking watermelons you can find. Bigger is better, but any size will do

Firm fruits and veggies that will hold on with the tip of a toothpick

Multicolored toothpicks

Uncle Sam party hat

GOT BUSY

To make faces, poke toothpicks into watermelon, leaving just enough of the tip to "stick" on the fruit or veggie. You may need a thimble.

SHOWTIME

Display the Uncle Watermelons in the middle of your red, white, and blue patio tablescape. Then ask your guests: Do we slice and serve the Uncle Watermelons or blow them up? Take a vote. You know you want to blow them up!

UNCLE WATERMELON CONTEST

This is the perfect way to begin the party. The more Uncle Watermelons, the merrier. Divide guests into teams. Have cut fruits and veggies on platters. Set a timer for 15 minutes and let the fun food crafting begin! Take a vote and have a prize for the winner.

PATRIOTS PARTYING IN POLYESTER

pose with the best Fourth of July centerpiece I've ever seen. He's like Mr. Potato Head but bigger, sweeter, and more patriotic. Whoever dreamed up this bicentennial-born veggie-faced fruit head deserves a big box of free fireworks. The very moment I saw this spirited centerpiece, I knew immediately he needed to become a new Fourth of July food-crafting tradition and be displayed proudly on that great day on every buffet table from coast to coast. What the jack-o'-lantern is to Halloween, Uncle Watermelon should be to July 4th.

SaFe and SaNe

The Chinese invented decorative explosives more than 1,000 years ago. Centuries later, Italians sent those spectacular sparks skyward. Today, Disney is the number-one fireworks consumer in the USA.

RED DEVIL FIREWORKS STAND, GLENDORA, CA
A United States flag and string of balloons fly high and proud over this plywood pyrotechnic pop-up shop–one of many that appear in the weeks before Independence Day in cities where recreational explosives are legal. Inside the Boy Scouts-sponsored, screened-in stand, stacks of explosives are sold separately or boxed in variety packs for your pleasure.

"8000 SPECIAL FIRECRACKER" explodes for a whopping 22 minutes. It's the specialty of the house at Roller Coaster Fireworks in Battle Mountain, NV, on the wide-open road between Yellowstone and Los Angeles.

1973 FIRECRACKER MOBILE My head is exploding over this clever cross between a firecracker and motor home celebrating "196 Years of Freedom." If you're gonna bomb the place, show up like you mean it—in this.

It's finally dark, everyone is gathered 'round, and the sparklers are sparkling. And who or what is that resting their head on the table? I have no idea! Is Dad taking a balsa-wood carving course? Is Mom practicing her butter-sculpting skills?

TRICK OR TREAT

Pick out a pumpkin, bust open those bags of candy, and get your masquerade on—it's Halloween, the edgiest night of the year. **Before we knife open our pick-o-the-patch, rip out his guts, carve him a face, place him on the porch, and ignite his inner glow, the burning question is: What are you going to be?** Which mask, what makeup, which costume will you cook up for the no-rules freak-fest frolic? **For the kids, the prize of the night of fright is candy for days. If you don't have the sweet stuff to hand them upon command, there'll be consequences.** But ones that come with a fair warning: Trick or treat!

JACK-O'-LANTERN LAND

THE FAMOUS PUMPKIN HOUSE

The world's largest hand-carved jack-o'-lantern display began in 1978 with just four lonely pumpkins on a front porch in Kenova, WV. In the true holiday spirit of "more is more," every year the homeowners added more, and more, and more. Today, the spellbinding, hypnotizing, and mesmerizing tradition continues with more than 3,000 pumpkins, each hand-carved and all aglow.

MOVE OVER, SANTA CLAUS AND PETER COTTONTAIL!
Make room for the Pumpkin King, the marvelous man in orange balancing a big, beautiful, heavy, high-gloss jack-o'-lantern on his head. His backdrop is breathtaking—just look at those giant jack-o'-lanterns with those gorgeous googly eyes. This is photo-op awesomeness like I've never ever seen before. Papier-mâché masters and set painters, please get to work—this Pumpkin King scene needs to come back to life!

HALLOWEEN ROYALTY

PUMPKIN KING
HOURS
Weekdays 6 PM to 9 PM

PIMP YOUR PUMPKIN

ASTRO-WEENIE Jack-o'-Lantern

Cut hole in top of pumpkin just big enough to hold a small bowl filled with your fave dip. Trim rim of the cut lid to fit over bowl. Complete **ASTRO-WEENIE** how-to guide on page 154.

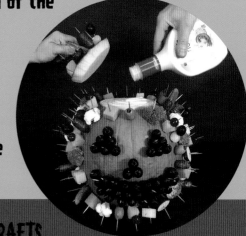

PUMPKIN ARTS & CRAFTS

Once a year, we get creative with a carving knife and test our glorified gourd-sculpting skills. But if you don't feel like hacking into pumpkin flesh, no problem—get out your paintbrush, get in touch with your inner Picasso, and paint your pumpkin. Or maybe you're a vegetarian and have some veggies to spare. Great! Skillfully stick them onto your pumpkin with toothpicks. Think Mr. Potato Head or, better yet, Uncle Watermelon (page 62).

PRETTY PUMPKIN IN PINK

"I can't believe I'm sitting here with Martha Stewart." That's what was going through my head all three times I guested on her TV show. The first segment we did together, I shared vintage Halloween slides from my collection. When I showed the one on the right, I politely asked, "Have you ever painted a pumpkin pink?" Without skipping a beat, she replied firmly, "I would *never* paint a pumpkin pink." Well, I sure would!

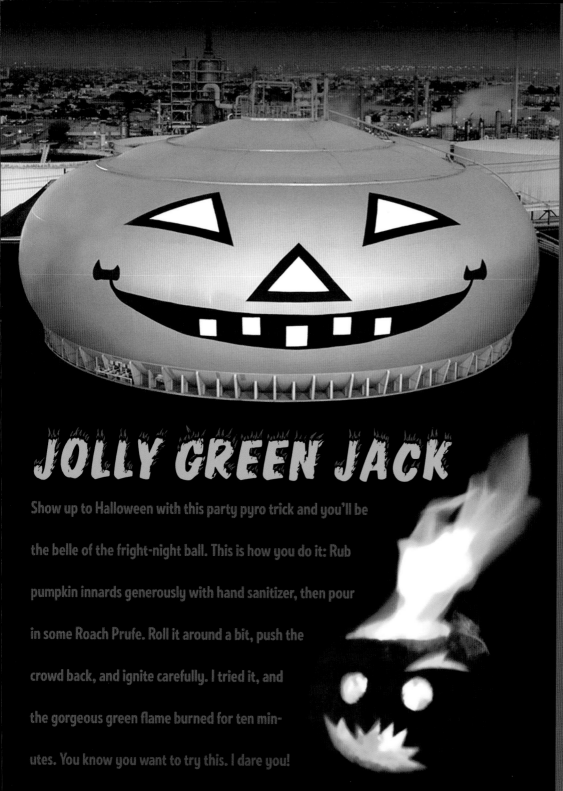

JOLLY GREEN JACK

Show up to Halloween with this party pyro trick and you'll be

the belle of the fright-night ball. This is how you do it: Rub

pumpkin innards generously with hand sanitizer, then pour

in some Roach Prufe. Roll it around a bit, push the

crowd back, and ignite carefully. I tried it, and

the gorgeous green flame burned for ten min-

utes. You know you want to try this. I dare you!

THE WORLD'S LARGEST JACK-O'-LANTERN

began by chance, in 1955, at the Union 76 oil refinery in Wilmington, CA, when a three-million-gallon oil tank was painted a brighter-than-expected shade of orange. Because it looked so much like a giant pump-kin, and it happened to be that jack-o'-lantern time of year, oil execs ordered that the job be finished with 18-foot-wide eyes and a 73-foot-wide smile. A super-sized Halloween tradition was born. When Phillips 66 took over the refinery, it adopted "Smilin' Jack," as the locals affec-tionately call him, and, thankfully, he still grins from ear to ear every Halloween to this day.

CASPER THE FRIENDLY PILLOWCASE GHOST

Apparently, the mom or dad, or whoever art-directed this old pillowcase, was channeling a little more Tweety Bird than Casper!

DISNEYLAND'S HAUNTED MANSION

The original concept drawings had the legendary antebellum home overgrown with wilted vines and dead trees. Walt rejected the run-down façade in favor of a pristine exterior. In 1961, Disneyland announced the grand opening would take place in 1963. But between the distractions, delays, and Walt's death, the iconic attraction didn't scare its first guest until 1969.

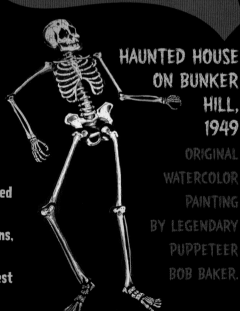

HAUNTED HOUSE ON BUNKER HILL, 1949

ORIGINAL WATERCOLOR PAINTING BY LEGENDARY PUPPETEER BOB BAKER.

HEARSES & HAUNTED HOUSES

DEATH RIDE

This rare 1960 Cadillac hearse special-bodied three-way landau by Eureka is gorgeous, but it gives me the creeps. With that said, when I go, please make sure I get to take my last ride in a midcentury modern mortuary mobile just like this one. And when I do go, do me a favor: Take the long way to the graveyard, and drive like a bat out of hell the whole way.

THE HOLIDAY OF HORROR JUST GOT SCARIER!

Slice into him and he oozes steaming ketchup. This meatloaf performs! Yes, his oozy, beefy little bod is filled with an entire squeeze bottle of ketchup. This roast rodent happened unexpectedly when I had a couple pounds of ground round hanging around and it just happened to be the season of scary. I gave him beady, bloodshot eyes with carved radishes stuffed with two green olives, a nose with a green olive, whiskers of spaghetti, kielbasa ears and tail, and to make him even creepier, chicken feet. Your guests will eat well, but they will be horrified!

GET THIS

3 lbs. of your grandma's meatloaf recipe, mixed and ready to be baked
2 red radishes
3 green olives

1 large kielbasa
Several strands of uncooked spaghetti
4 of the biggest chicken feet you can find
1 large squeeze bottle of ketchup

GET BUSY

Shape, form, and sculpt meatloaf mix into a hollow rat's body big enough to fill with a whole squeeze bottle of ketchup. Place on foil-covered baking tray. Add face, feet, and tail and bake at 350° for 60 minutes, or until a probing meat thermometer reads 170°, or...until he looks like he's charred to death!

SHOWTIME

Keep your meat rat in the oven on warm until you're ready to serve the little beady-eyed beast. When it's time for the dinner bell to ring, gather everyone around the oven, propose a toast to him, and say, "Meatloaf of Rat is served piping hot." As you slowly open the oven door and reveal him, scream, pause, and then stab him in the back and watch him bleed ketchup all over. Serve with hot buttered onion rolls. Let the frightful feast begin!

CROSS-DRESSERS

COMIC STRIPPER

HALLOWEEN is the one day of the year on which we give one another unlimited license to assume the identity of someone or something else. Any manner of fashion fantasy, devilish or delightful dress-up disguise, or combination thereof will do. Only your imagination and creative skills can hold you back from scaring up an inspired costume.

WHAT ARE YOU GOING TO BE?

PHYLLIS DILLER

MEDIEVAL PRINCESS & VAMP

BRIDEZILLA, COUSIN IT, THE SH... ED ...ONG

76

MYSTERY MAN

THE MARTIANS

FEATHER LADY

HEADLESS MAN & WITCHY WOMAN

FRANKENSTEIN

CIGARETTE GIRL

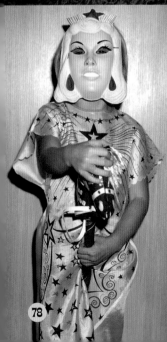

Collegeville Costumes

BRIGHT FOR NIGHT

FLAME RETARDED

Quality Costumes

COLORFUL MASKS

WIDE-VISION EYE-HOLES

OFFICIAL COPYRIGHT Costume

PLASTIC & POLYESTER

BEN COOPER AND COLLEGEVILLE were once the biggest names in boxed costumes. Collegeville started in the late 1920s in Pennsylvania as an American flag maker. Its first costumes were Santa Claus and Uncle Sam made with leftover red and white flag fabric. Ben Cooper was a costume designer for the legendary Ziegfeld Follies when he began manufacturing children's Halloween costumes in 1937 in Brooklyn, NY. By the 1950s, between the rival companies, virtually every scary and pop culture character was available. By the early 1980s, the demand for this type of disguise diminished, and both companies quietly disappeared into the dark of night.

COLLEGEVILLE COSTUMES

RIDE WITH THE COLORFUL LINE FOR HALLOWEEN SALES

FULL COLOR TV FOR 1966

TO SEE OR NOT TO

SUPER-SIZE ME

Clearly it wouldn't be easy to see out of Elmer Fudd's eyebrow, Colonel Burp's forehead, or a giant baby's tonsils. These sensational yet sadly short-lived costumes, intended for "large children and teens," were part of a collection called Mask-A-Rama introduced in 1960 by Collegeville.

SEE

KOOKY SPOOKS

After a couple of decades of kids complaining that they couldn't see out of their Halloween masks, some ingenious toy designer in the mid-'60s apparently came up with these inflatable figures headdresses in the late '70s. They were manufactured by a beach ball company.

GIVE ME
CANDY OR
ELSE!
IF YOU DON'T HAVE
THE SWEET STUFF,
FRESH FRUIT,
HOMEMADE
COOKIES, ROASTED
PEANUTS, OR COPPER
PENNIES WILL DO.
THANK YOU!

TRICK
OR TREAT

Giant vintage candy
carrier rolling along in
the legendary Anaheim
Halloween Parade,
Anaheim,
CA.

49¢ 50 SUCKERS

TRICK-R-TRIM HAUNTED HOUSE

WHATCHU GET?

Valentine's Day, Easter, and Christmas were well established as candycentric by the 1920s. But it wasn't until the 1950s that Halloween hopped on the candy conveyer belt and became sugar dependent.

THE KING OF CANDY

In 1904, candyman extraordinaire Emil J. Brachs invested his life savings into a "one kettle" candy store, called Brach's Palace of Sweets, in Chicago, IL. By streamlining the candy-making operation, his signature sweets sold for less than half the price of his competitors. By the late 1940s, he was the King of Candy, producing more of the sweet stuff than any other manufacturer in the world.

PSYCHEDELIC CANDY CAKE

Chocolate lovers, start lining up. You know a psychedelic cake slathered in milk chocolate frosting covered with bite-size pieces of Butterfingers, Reese's, Milky Ways, Whoppers, Snickers, Kit Kats, Twix, Almond Joys, Mounds, and M&Ms (plain and peanut) is more than finger-lickin' good, it's a gut-altering experience.

Food coloring fanatics, this one is for you, too. No apologies for too much of a good thing here. Have no fear of color. More is more, and brighter is better!

COSMIC KALEIDOSCOPE OF COLOR, CAKE, CHOCOLATE, AND CANDY!

85

GET THIS

4 boxes white cake mix

7 bottles food coloring

6 tubs Hershey's milk chocolate frosting
(dark chocolate works, too)

Regular-size bag of each of these Halloween candies:

BUTTERFINGER · REESE'S · MILKY WAY · SNICKERS · KIT KAT
TWIX · ALMOND JOY · MOUNDS · M&MS · PEANUT M&MS · WHOPPERS

GET BUSY

COLORIZING CAKE

Divide batter, mixed according to box instructions, into five parts. Mix in food coloring. Don't hold back. Put colorized batter into squeeze bottles. Spray five cake pans with PAM. Line bottoms of cake pans with parchment paper. Flour sides of pans.

To create psychedelic cake effect, squeeze about ½ cup batter in concentric circles into the center of a cake pan. Repeat until each cake pan is about ¾ full. No two layers should look alike. Spooning batter into cake pans will not achieve the desired effect—it must be squeezed. Bake according to box instructions. Use the classic "toothpick test" to make sure cakes are thoroughly baked.

FROSTING, FILLING & STUDDING

Freeze candy overnight. Unwrap each piece and cut with scissors into 2 or 3 bite-size chunks, saving the candy crumbs. Freeze again.

Stack and fill each cake layer with generous spread of frosting mixed with cut chunks of candy. Refrigerate before crumb coating the sides. Coat with reserved candy crumbs and refrigerate.

Frost cake exterior generously. Carefully hand-place remaining chunks of candy in frosting until sides and top of cake are covered. Sampling as you go, of course!

SHOWTIME!

Gather your costumed guests around the cake with festive flair and fanfare. Wave your vintage electric knife around like you've just seen THE TEXAS CHAINSAW MASSACRE. Present your psycho-cocoa cake with wit and whimsy. Then hit the cake, start hacking away, and serve it screaming... it's HALLOWEEN!

Pass the Gravy

PREHEAT THE OVEN, STUFF THE BUTTERBALL AND SPICE THE PUMPKIN—
it's Thanksgiving, the most famous dinner day of the year. We give thanks by stuffing ourselves with stuffing, along with an abundance of other golden-buttery-brown delicious dishes. The flavorful feast is mostly meat and mush, and the gravy makes it even mushier. This is the dinner that doesn't discriminate against people who don't have teeth— mashed potatoes, yams, stuffing, pumpkin pie, and cranberry sauce require only gums to eat. Perfect for great-grandma and baby alike! Now please pass the gravy!

The annual tradition

began in 1924 as the Macy's Christmas Day parade—

even though it was held on Thanksgiving. The procession of floats

and caged Central Park Zoo animals drew masses to kick off Macy's holiday shopping season. In 1927, Macy's

replaced the live animals with giant character balloons. Between 1928 and 1933, the inflated spectacles were

released when they reached the end of the parade route, floating away into the wild blue, and the treasure hunt

began. Macy's offered rewards to those who found the deflated balloons. In 1947, MIRACLE ON 34TH STREET

introduced the parade to movie audiences worldwide, and the very next year it was broadcast on television for

Macy's THANKSGIVING

the first time. Not only
does Macy's claim to be the
"world's largest department store," it can also claim to
be the world's second-largest consumer of helium. The US govern-
ment is the first, and people who want to talk funny are the third.

DAY PARADE

Insist on...

PAVO

BIG BREASTED TURKEYS

AT ALL *Ralphs* MARKETS

Breasty Billboard

This gives "turkey breast" a whole new meaning! Everyone knows that turkeys have big breasts, but we don't usually think of them as going topless. I'd never ever seen a training bra strapped onto a buxom fowl, but I have now, and it's about time. All turkeys should be shipped to supermarkets wearing brassieres. Let's shake up our beloved Thanksgiving dinner tradition by serving our plump roast turkeys wearing bras. Imagine the surprise and delight of your thankful dinner guests. Once the turkey-bra brouhaha blows over, don't skip a beat—bring out a big, juicy Virginia baked ham wearing a pair of panties. Not you, the ham! Your Turkey Day denizens will be delighted, and this holiday will never be the same. Thanksgiving is destined to become a big underwear party!

Turkey Lurkey

TECHNICOLOR TURKEYS

GOZZI'S TURKEY FARM, GUILFORD, CT

Thanksgiving's most colorful tradition began in 1940 on the day Mrs. Gozzi hand-dyed a dozen lucky turkeys to amuse children while their parents picked their poultry. The rainbow flock was a smash sensation, and the Gozzi family has been tinting toms ever since.

GOZZI'S TURKEY FARM

ASTRO-WEENIE
ROAST TOM TURKEY DOG

Looking for a flavor-filled alternative to white or dark meat? Think pink! Try this meatloaf stuck with skewered hot dogs, cocktail weenies, and fresh cranberries. I didn't mean to create this, it just happened. I just did it, and you can, too. I double dare you!

GET BUSY

Bake meatloaf until well done. Remove from pan and cool to room temperature. Center meatloaf on lined baking sheet. Cut kielbasa to look like a turkey head and neck. Attach to body with toothpicks. Finish body with toothpicked cranberries and hot dog tips. Attach wiener wings with toothpicks. For the big tail-feather flourish, arrange random skewered foot-long and bun-length dogs with cranberries.

GET THIS

3 lbs. of your grandma's meatloaf recipe, mixed and placed in loaf pan

Foil-lined baking sheet

1 kielbasa sausage

1 box round toothpicks

1 bag fresh cranberries

2 packages each foot-long, bun-length, and li'l smoky turkey dogs

2 bags skewer sticks

SHOWTIME

Have your wild weenie bird sitting front and center on the first table your Thanksgiving guests will see as they enter your gorgeous home. Make sure the lighting is just right, because you want those hot dogs to glow and the cranberries to sparkle when they all take selfies with it. Later that night, when everybody gets the munchies, shove it in the oven at 325° for a few minutes, until the weenies start to toast. Then get out the mustard, buns, and beer. It will be a late-night hot dog snack memory for a lifetime!

A FUN, FESTIVE THANKSGIVING APPETIZER CENTERPIECE!

This big ol' turkey-shaped cheese, cracker, and salami platter is sure to sensationalize your big, birdy day. It's the perfect excuse to go on a shopping spree at the supermarket. Who doesn't love filling up a cart with a carefully curated selection of brightly boxed, salty, crunchy, crispy, cracker flavor bombs, bricks of cheese, and a tube of cured meat!

GET THIS

1 large salami
1 large block Velveeta
2 bricks cheddar cheese
1 box saltines
1 box Triscuits
1 box Cheez-Its
1 box Ritz Crackers
1 box Wheat Thins
1 box Chicken in a Biskit
1 can spray cheese
1 green olive with pimento pupil
1 slice red bell pepper
1 24-inch platter

SNACKS-GIVING GOBBLER PLATTER

GET BUSY

To start your cheese and cracker crafting, carefully carve salami to create a one-piece neck and head and two little legs with feet. Lovingly form room-temperature Velveeta into a half ball to make the body. Place on platter. Cut cheddar and remaining salami into ¼-inch slices for feathers. Starting on the outside of the platter, arrange sliced cheese, salami, and crackers, layering in toward the body. To be safe, you can "glue" the first outside layer of Ritz Crackers with spray cheese to hold them in place. Feather the Velveeta body by pushing crackers into it. Finish with carved salami feet, an olive eye, and red pepper gobbler, and voila, you've done it.

SHOWTIME

Before your guests begin attacking your Snacksgiving Gobbler Platter, give thanks to the li'l cheese and cracker snacker, and to every other blessing in your sweet life, and let the gobble, gobble, gobbling begin!

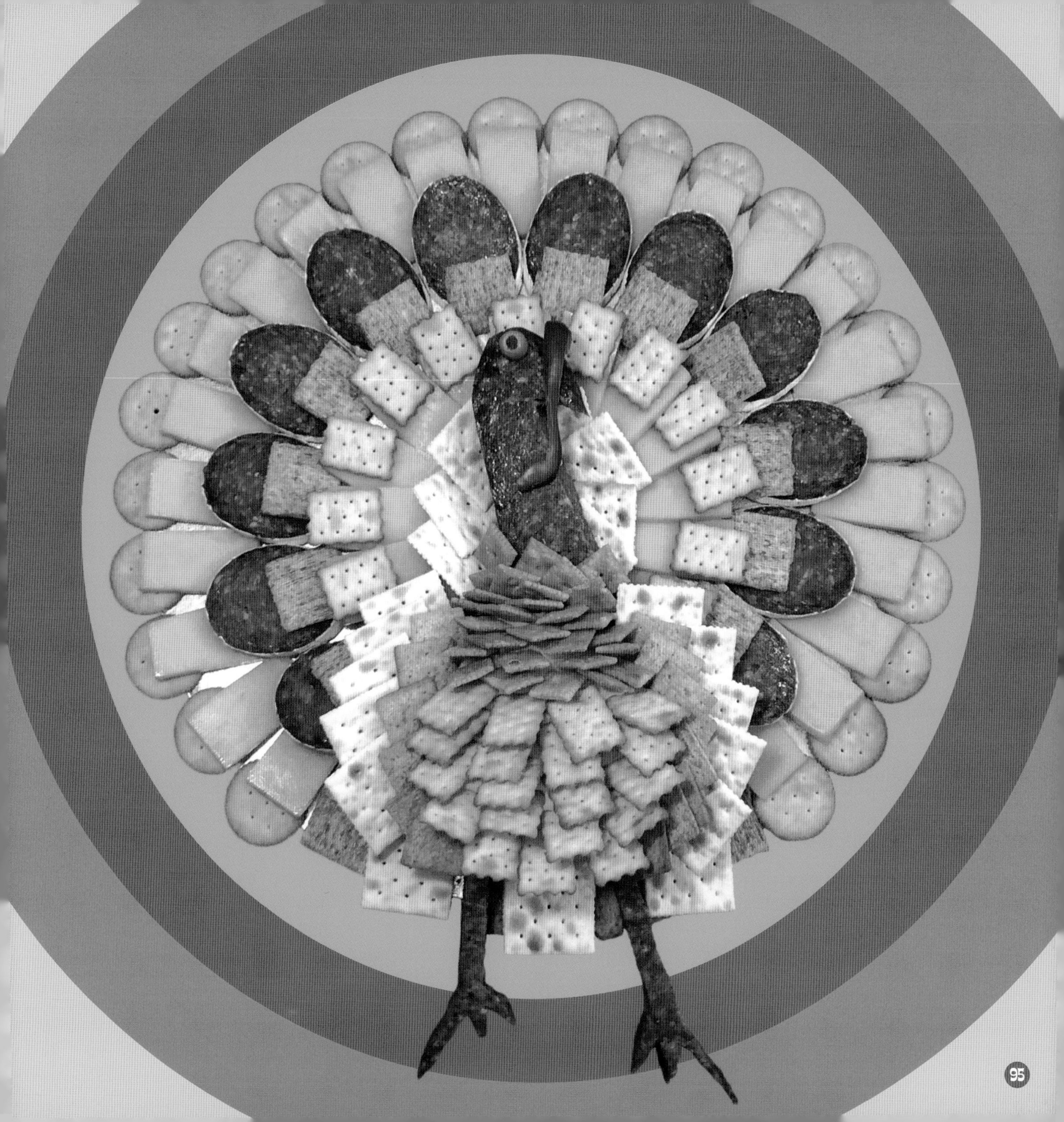

Dinner Is Served

WHO'S GONNA CARVE THE TURKEY?

The table is set, the guests are gathered, and the bird is roasted. Dinner is served with all the trimmings—even a mouthwatering molded ring of two-tone Jell-O. The mini hula doll provides entertainment with a plate dance. This is the "say cheese" moment just before the flavorful beast is cut into slices, bits, and pieces. Clearly, the gent at the head of the table is the right man for the job. He has perfect turkey-carving poise: elbows out and fingers one-quarter of an inch apart, except for his very proper pinkie. Now who gets the lucky wishbone?

"The Dress-Like-the-Décor Sisters."

I can hear their conversation now, "Do you want to be the drapes or the tablecloth?"

We might as well just get it out in the open: Thanksgiving could use some new traditions. Dressing like the décor should be one of them. You don't want to be the drapes or the tablecloth? No problem. Be the sofa or a side chair. And don't forget the kids–they can be the throw pillows.

DINNER OFFICIALLY DITCHED THE DINING ROOM IN 1953 when the famous frozen-food factory introduced the TV dinner. A quick-thinking salesman cooked up the idea after a company purchasing agent made a monumental mistake by over-ordering a whopping 260 tons of Thanksgiving turkeys. To save the day, they filled 5,000 aluminum airline-food trays with the turkey and two savory sides. Bingo! A pop-culture icon was born, and dinner would be never be the same.

Swanson's
TV Dinner

Swanson **T.V DINNER**

QUICK FROZEN
TURKEY DINNER
JUST HEAT AND SERVE!

The most important question on Thanksgiving Day: How to serve the Cranberry Sauce?
Leaning or Laying?

Honey-blond cabinets and flowery barbed-wire wallpaper provide an inviting backdrop for a dear mother and her milk-drinking, Clark Kent-wannabe son. The dinner looks delicious, but I can't take my eyes off the leaning tower of cranberry sauce. We call it "cranberry sauce," but there's nothing saucy about this ruby-red turkey flavor enhancer. It's more of a jelly that's molded like Jell-O. It even jiggles like Jell-O. It's the only food we serve in the shape of the tin can it came in. And who thought of the

unlikely combo of cranberry sauce and turkey in the first place? The same pilgrim who thought of serving mint jelly and leg of lamb? And exactly what is a "cran" anyway? Turns out it's short for "crane." Early Americans thought the plant's flower resembled the head of the lanky bird, so they named the berries cranberries. Whether your bird-head-berry tin-can mold is falling over or lying down, we all know that Thanksgiving dinner just wouldn't be Thanksgiving dinner without it.

Pumpkin Pie

Once you've had your pie, you've crossed the Thanksgiving finish line—you can go home now, thank you very much. Don't forget your leftovers! The namesake main ingredient of this sweet, spiced sensation is in a patch all its own. From mini to massive, these harvest-time darlings grow in a wider variety of sizes than any other fruit or vegetable. Speaking of, we don't really think of them as fruits or vegetables—they are simply pumpkins, the superstar of the squash family. But we never call them squash, because then you'd have to say "squash pie," and nobody wants to eat that.

Reddi Whip

Wonderfully whipped cream comes fresh from the nifty nozzle of a pressurized aerosol can with just the flip of a fingertip. It's a midcentury modern miracle! The technology for this kitchen convenience was originally invented for bug spray. In 1948, canners replaced the insecticide with cream, and it's been pumpkin pie's best friend ever since.

just a SLIVER

World's Largest Pumpkin Pie

It's created every year by Lindsey's Bakery for Ohio's epic Circleville pumpkin show. Looks like they burned this one a bit. Oh well. It's six feet across and has 40 pounds of sugar in it. After being drooled over for four festive days, no one in town will touch it. Thankfully it doesn't go to waste. As soon as the pumpkin party is over, it's served up to some very lucky pigs. Oink, oink!

THANKSGIVING
with an
EXOTIC TWIST!

TIKI TURKEY DINNER PARTY

Tired of the same ol' traditional Thanksgiving menu year after year? Mix it up! Make it fun and festive by giving every dish an exotic flavor twist. Replacing the roasted bird with a turkey meatloaf shaped like a tiki gives "carving the turkey" a whole new meaning. Mangos make cranberry sauce sing. Cornbread stuffing becomes Hawaiian bread stuffing with diced ham and pineapple. Yams get dressed up with bananas and Kahlúa before being topped with toasted marshmallows and crushed macadamia nuts. Coconut curry revolutionizes the classic green bean casserole. Request that guests wear vintage Hawaiian-style attire, and greet each one with a lei. After dessert, do the limbo. How low can you go… after a Tiki Turkey Dinner?

the TUR-KIKI COCKTAIL

Every great party calls for a special tiki drink. In honor of the Tiki Turkey Dinner, I created the tongue-curling Tur-Kiki.

Because it's Thanksgiving, I wanted to try to make pumpkin Polynesian and turn that into a cocktail, but it just wasn't working, so I happily opted for Turkey Day's other most popular flavors, cranberry and apple. I mixed in some yummy coconut cream, and finished it with a sassy splash of maraschino cherry juice right out of the jar.

GET THIS

4 ounces coconut cream

4 ounces spiced rum

4 ounces Martinelli's Cranberry Apple Sparkling Cider

Cinnamon sticks

1 ounce maraschino cherry syrup (out of the jar)

GET BUSY

Shake coconut cream and spiced rum together with ice. Pour over Martinelli's on the rocks, stir with a cinnamon stick, splash with maraschino syrup, and gleefully garnish as you wish. Mix up a big batch, fill your Tiki Turkey Meatloaf mugs to the brim, and propose a thankful tiki toast! **CHEERS!**

the TUR-KIKI KIDDIE COCKTAIL

Make sure to mix up a rum-less batch for the little ones.

the TUR-KIKI GARNISH

Create a space-age starburst by spiking multicolored toothpicks into a maraschino cherry.

TIKI TURKEY MEATLOAF MUG

When I cooked up the idea for Tiki Turkey Meatloaf and wanted to turn it into a limited-edition tiki mug, I went to master tiki mug maker and all-around nice guy Mikel Parton, of MP Ceramics in Santa Cruz, CA. Skillfully, he handcrafted each Tiki Turkey Meatloaf Mug with heart and soul. The finished product with its bright maraschino cherry eyes and happy pineapple smile, sold like Dole Whip on a hot day at Disneyland. The mighty meaty mugs are now prized collectibles and collecting dust on tiki bar shelves from coast to coast and several points beyond.

GET THIS

1 can pineapple chunks

1 jar maraschino cherries

6 lbs. of your grandma's meatloaf recipe, mixed and ready to bake

10 cups stiff mashed potatoes

1 10-by-14-inch disposable roasting pan

GET BUSY

Drain pineapple and cherries in fridge overnight. Toss pineapple with a few drops of yellow food coloring.

Fill roasting pan with meatloaf mix. Channel your inner tiki carver and start shaping. Think Easter Island. Smooth the meat's surface with water.

Bake at 350° until a probing meat thermometer reads 170°, about 1 hour.

Remove from pan and cool just enough to lean him onto a tall glass fixed in a bed of mashed potatoes.

Give him a face and flattering frame with maraschino cherries and pineapple chunks stuck with multicolored toothpicks.

EASTER ISLAND DINNER

If you don't want to turn your Thanksgiving dinner into a Polynesian party, make it for Easter!

TIKI TURKEY MEATLOAF

HAWAIIAN BREAD STUFFING

GET THIS

1 can pineapple chunks

48 Hawaiian bread rolls

2 sticks salted butter

2 cups each: finely chopped onion, finely chopped celery, finely chopped carrots

¼ cup soy sauce

2 small cans Campbell's chicken stock

4 cups diced ham

2 teaspoons each: sage, thyme, poultry seasoning

GET BUSY

Drain pineapple overnight. Tear bread into small pieces. In large skillet, sauté onions, celery, and carrots in butter until onions are translucent. Add soy sauce, stock, ham, seasonings, and pineapple. Combine mixture with bread in greased baking dish. Cover with foil and bake at 350° for 40 minutes. Remove foil and bake uncovered 5 more minutes until crunchy golden brown on top.

YAMANANALUA

GET THIS

1 stick salted butter

3 ripe bananas, mashed

½ cup brown sugar

1 cup Kahlúa

3 40-ounce cans yams

2 cups mini marshmallows

1 cup chopped macadamia nuts

VOLCANO MASHED POTATOES & LAVA GRAVY

Don't forget to serve your mashed potatoes in the shape of a volcano. Refer to your gravy as "lava." Stir well, no one wants lumpy lava.

GET BUSY

Sauté bananas and brown sugar in the butter until mixture bubbles. Remove from heat and add Kahlúa. Pour mixture over well-drained yams. Transfer to greased baking dish, cover with foil, and bake at 350° for 30 minutes. Remove foil, top with marshmallows and macadamia nuts, and bake uncovered until marshmallows are gooey-toasty, about 5 more minutes.

COCONUT CURRY GREEN BEAN CASSEROLE

GET THIS

8 small cans French-cut green beans
1 small can cream of mushroom soup
1 jar coconut curry simmer sauce
½ cup crunchy peanut butter
1 large can French fried onion rings

GET BUSY

Drain beans overnight. Blend soup, coconut curry, and peanut butter. Combine with beans. Place in greased baking dish, cover with foil, and bake at 350° for 30 minutes. Remove foil, top with onion rings, and bake uncovered 5 more minutes.

CRANMANGOBERRY SAUCE

GET THIS

1 can whole cranberry sauce
1 cup dried cranberries
1 cup fresh or frozen
   chopped mango

GET BUSY

Combine ingredients in bowl, chill overnight, and serve.
Make a few days ahead and it's even better.

SHOWTIME

Crank up the Martin Denny, cue the hula dancers, and blow the conch shell—it's Tiki Turkey Dinnertime. Introduce your guests to each dish, and then, with the spirit of an island war chant, present your Moai meatloaf masterpiece with grace and gratitude. Set him in the center of the table and let the feeding frenzy begin! Don't forget to fire up the tiki torches.

The Most Time

TOSS THE TINSEL, egg the nog, cue the carolers, and plug in the color wheel—it's Christmas, the most dynamic, decorated, and documented holiday of the year.

Wonderful of the Year

What started 2,000-plus years ago as the Oh Holy Silent Night exploded into the ultimate expression of our blessed mass-consumerism culture. The season of Santa is capitalism pimped out to the max and finely tuned into a wildly orchestrated symphony of sing-a-long shopping sprees and traditions colliding into a fever-pitched frenzy of festivities. Every year the calendar's grand finale starts earlier and earlier, gets bigger and bigger, and lasts longer and longer than the 12 days of Christmas. Halloween, Thanksgiving, and Christmas are beginning to morph into one big flavor-filled pumpkin-cranberry-peppermint feast. You simply can't escape the ho ho ho holiday. The evidence is everywhere. But when it's all over, whether it's been a white one, a blue one, a holly jolly one, or a merry little one, Christmas really is the most wonderful time of the year.

DENVER CITY &
COUNTY BUILDING,
DENVER, CO, 1960

Santa's Village
A Christmas Miracle

YOU HAVE ARRIVED AT SANTA'S VILLAGE, the most colorful, candy-coated Christmasland theme park in the world. Nestled on 15 prime acres of enchanted forest in Lake Arrowhead, CA, the park opened in 1955, six weeks before Disneyland. The over-the-top, cartoon-like storybook buildings were built from logs cut from local pines and embellished inside and out with clever details crafted by local artisans. This whimsical winter wonderland was designed to keep the legend of Santa Claus alive throughout the year, but ironically it was open every day BUT Christmas. Santa's Village enjoyed decades of success, including two spin-off locations, one in Santa Cruz, CA, and the other in Dundee, IL.

(CONTINUES ON PAGE 110)

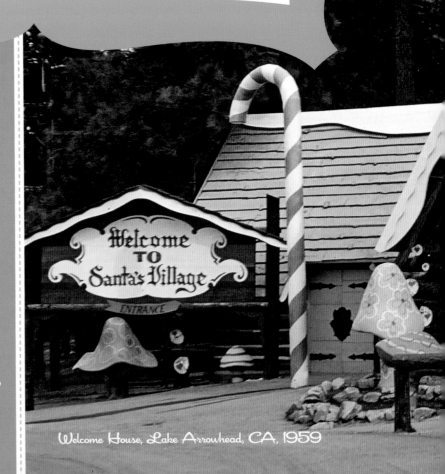

Welcome House, Lake Arrowhead, CA, 1959

(CONTINUED FROM PAGE 108)

After years of operational challenges, the park closed unceremoniously in 1998. I was lucky to be there just a few days before they shuttered the Welcome House for good...or so we thought.

In mid-2016 I heard rumblings that Santa's Village might be reopening and that the rides had been sold off but the buildings remained. Thankfully they hadn't blown over, burned down, or been eaten by termites.

Could this rumor be true? I sped up the hill to investigate. The place seemed deserted. Everything was locked up. The first thing I saw was a vintage bumble-bee monorail car sitting in front of the Welcome House. I made a beeline right for it. Out of nowhere, a man appeared and said, "Sir, you're going to have to leave, this is private property."

"Can't I just take a pic with the Bumblebee?" I got my pic and was escorted off the property.

Much to everyone's surprise and against all odds, Santa's Village did in fact reopen, lovingly reimagined as Skypark at Santa's Village, just in time for Christmas 2017.

Shortly after the triumphant grand reopening, I was welcomed with open arms and given the grand tour. The style and spirit of the reincarnated park is spellbinding. If ever there was a true Christmas miracle, this is it!

THE FROZEN NORTH POLE

was the centerpiece and crowning touch of Santa's Village. The ice on the pole never melted, no matter how hot it got. Just don't lick it!

THE WHIRLING CHRISTMAS TREE

was just like the Dumbo ride at Disneyland, round and round and up and down, only instead of elephants there were ornaments!

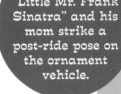

"Little Mr. Frank Sinatra" and his mom strike a post-ride pose on the ornament vehicle.

PAST & PRESENT

MAGIC MUSHROOMS

The original Santa's Village was home to many rides and attractions, but it's the giant striped and polka-dot cement mushrooms that I remember the most. I only visited the park with my family once when I was a kid. For years afterward, I pestered my parents, begging them to landscape our front yard with giant mushrooms. It didn't happen. Thankfully, I can enjoy the new and vintage mushrooms at today's Santa Village.

THE WORLD'S ONLY BUMBLEBEE MONORAIL

Families enjoyed the bee's-eye view of the park. The giant black-and-yellow-striped stinger has nothing to do with Christmas, but who cares? There are no rules at Santa's Village. The monorail wasn't included in the redo, but a couple of the bumblebee cars are on display and make a great photo op!

PAST & PRESENT

Santa even had his own train! All aboard for a scenic **MINIATURE RAILROAD** trip through the Enchanted Forest.

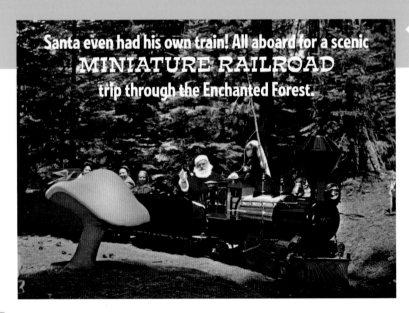

Ticket to Ride

Dashing through the thrilling ice caverns on the CANDY CANE SLEIGH pulled by Santa's reindeers. Where's Rudolph?

Young drivers could take the wheel of a mini mock ANTIQUE FORD MODEL T, the most up-to-date and modern transportation in the village.

Fantasy princess wannabes rode like Cinderella in her pretty PUMPKIN COACH, drawn by a cute quartet of white ponies.

A Taste of SANTA'S VILLAGE

GINGERBREAD SHOP

Long before food trucks, Santa's Village had a food trailer. In 1961, the village bakers decided to take their gingerbread on the road. They built a bakery-on-wheels disguised as a pink midcentury modern gingerbread house. To this day it's still making the rounds at fairs and festivals, serving their famous fresh-baked gingerbread made from the original recipe. You can find the Gingerbread Shop at the Del Mar Fair in June and July, and at the Mission Inn during the Christmas season.

GINGERBREAD SHOP
CAKES
COOKIES
COFFEE

GOOD WITCH'S BAKERY

PAST & PRESENT

Twin gingerbread men stuck in pink stucco frosting, heart-shaped shutters, and a cookie-covered outdoor oven make this the sweetest bakery ever built. The stucco contractor deserves a major award—that frosting looks real. Of all the buildings in the park, the Good Witch's Bakery is my very favorite. It's also the one I was most surprised to see again when I visited the new Santa's Village. All these years later, now frosted white, it still looks good enough to eat. But when the time comes for a fresh coat of paint on that fabulous frosting, rest assured I'll be strongly suggesting they think pink!

Rustic rough-cut pine, polka-dot curtains, giant jingle bells, and Easter egg-colored accents give the MILL WHEEL TOY SHOP boundless charm and enchantment. Elves sold high-quality, made-in-the-USA toy cars and trucks, and in the coveted corner spot is the revolutionary remote-control Robert the Robot: "He walks, talks, and picks things up!"

Find the serenity of the season in the CHAPEL OF THE LITTLE SHEPHERD, the most peaceful place in the village.

Employees, colorfully costumed as elves, sold tickets and souvenirs, served food and refreshments, and operated the rides... with bells on!

WE ARE Santa's Elves

PRINCESS EVERGREEN strikes a beautiful bow-and-arrow pose in front of the restored and reimagined Santa's House.

I can't think of any other place I'd rather have my picture taken with Santa than the new Skypark at Santa's Village.

PAST & PRESENT

Santa's House

Candlestick shutters, bells hanging from beams, and a giant antique clock counting down the months till Christmas adorned Santa's House. Inside, kids checked to see if their names were in the "good book" and posed for portaits with the man himself.

Santa Claus House

NORTH POLE, AK, 1970

IN THE HOPE OF LURING A TOY FACTORY that could label its toys "Made at the North Pole," the town of Davis, AK, changed its name to North Pole in 1953. The toy factory never happened, but luckily the Santa Claus House did. Santa is there to this day, awaiting your arrival.

BRONNER'S

FRANKENMUTH, MI, 1969

SANTA HAS BEEN THE OFFICIAL parking lot greeter at the "World's Largest Christmas Store," furnishing holiday décor since 1945.

SUPER-SIZED SANTAS

**BURDINES
DEPARTMENT
STORE**

MIAMI, FL, 1957

ALL AGLOW AND ANIMATED with more than a mile of neon in seven sizzling colors and standing six stories tall, this is the largest and most electrified Santa Claus the world has ever known. Between 1950 and 1960, he illuminated the night, perched on the pedestrian bridge next to Burdines, the department store famous for "sunshine fashions." This super-sized Santa so richly deserves to be reincarnated for a new generation. Imagine how wonderful it would be to bask in the glow of this electrifying midcentury masterpiece.

SAVING SANTA

Carpenteria, CA

The DATE SHOP · HOME MADE BRITTLES

AND

ERE IS WHERE YOU GET SANTA'S FAMOUS DATE SHAKES

SANDWICHES

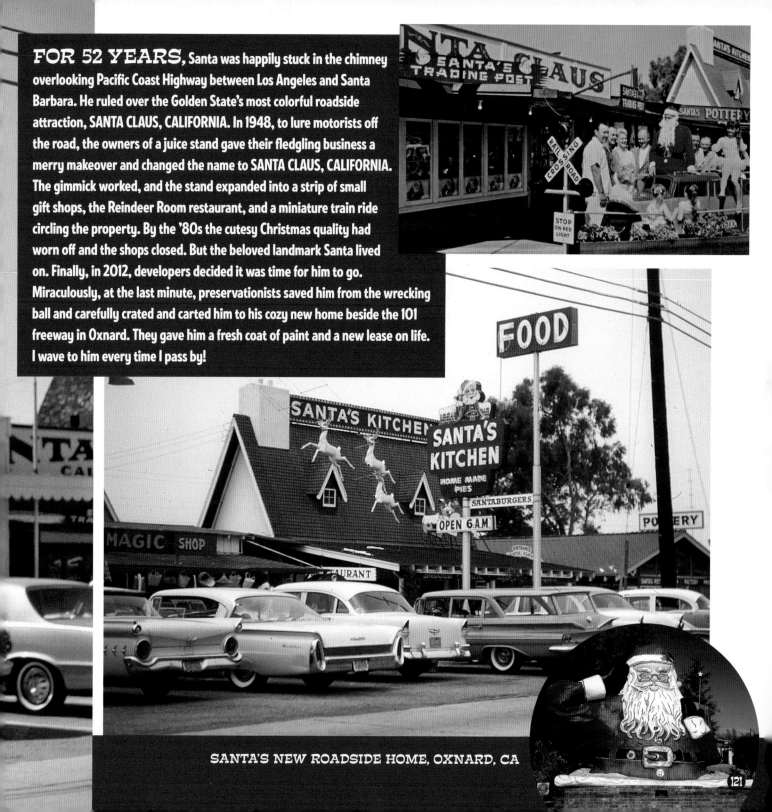

FOR 52 YEARS, Santa was happily stuck in the chimney overlooking Pacific Coast Highway between Los Angeles and Santa Barbara. He ruled over the Golden State's most colorful roadside attraction, SANTA CLAUS, CALIFORNIA. In 1948, to lure motorists off the road, the owners of a juice stand gave their fledgling business a merry makeover and changed the name to SANTA CLAUS, CALIFORNIA. The gimmick worked, and the stand expanded into a strip of small gift shops, the Reindeer Room restaurant, and a miniature train ride circling the property. By the '80s the cutesy Christmas quality had worn off and the shops closed. But the beloved landmark Santa lived on. Finally, in 2012, developers decided it was time for him to go. Miraculously, at the last minute, preservationists saved him from the wrecking ball and carefully crated and carted him to his cozy new home beside the 101 freeway in Oxnard. They gave him a fresh coat of paint and a new lease on life. I wave to him every time I pass by!

SANTA'S NEW ROADSIDE HOME, OXNARD, CA

ARE YOU A BELIEVER?

I was born a realist, so it didn't take long for me to figure out that there was no Santa. For Christmas when I was about five, we left cookies and milk out for Santa. About an hour after I went to bed, I got up to see if he'd been there and eaten the cookies, only to find my dad enjoying them. That was the moment I knew Santa wasn't coming to our house, or anybody's house. I wanted to believe he delivered gifts to every kid on the planet in one night with nothing but a sleigh and eight flying reindeer, one with a light-up nose leading the way, but I just couldn't. I wasn't buying this way-too-far-fetched fairy tale. My revelation was met with strict instructions not to say a word about this to my cousins, who were all still believers.

Hey, SANTa!

CARDBOARD CHRISTMAS

Christmas is all about family. But who needs a real one when you can put a fake one in the window to fool the neighbors? Santa doesn't mind!

SCARY SANTAS

CHUCKIE SANTA

How'd they get that Chuckie to look at the little girl like that? And how'd they get him to assume the "I'm-about-to-strangle-you pose?"

Santa's helper forgot her elf costume, but that doesn't stop her from handing the little girl a gift. She protests by putting her finger down her throat. The little boy, wearing floods and saggy socks, is very brave. He looks Santa right in the eye, probably to ask for a toy gun!

Christmas Meatloaf of Santa Claus

The Merriest Main Dish of Them All!

Bell peppers cut into holly leaves, baby grape tomatoes, and green olives surround this well-seasoned Santa. His beard, brows, and fur trim are made from mashed potatoes. Seasoned tomato paste glazes his meat hat. And, of course, he has a cherry-tomato Rudolf the Red-Nosed Reindeer nose. This merry meat-and-potatoes portrait in a pan was destined to happen. Serving Santa is exactly what Christmas has been waiting for: a new meaty main-dish tradition, picture-perfect for office, white-elephant, and post-caroling holiday parties.

Who can resist those big boiled-egg-and-olive eyes?

GET THIS

3 green bell peppers
1 red bell pepper
3 lbs. of your grandma's meatloaf recipe, mixed and ready to be baked
2 hard-boiled eggs
1 green olive, sliced in half
1 slice ham
6 cups mashed potatoes
Large pastry bag with ½-inch star tip
1 cherry tomato
1 small can seasoned tomato paste
1 cup baby grape tomatoes

GET BUSY

Cut green peppers into holly leaves and trim a piece of the top of the red pepper into a smile to serve as Santa's mouth. Shape happy face and hat with meatloaf mixture. Insert eggs for eyes and red pepper for mouth, and finish with sliced olives so he can see if you're naughty or nice. Cut ham into arcs to serve as eyelids. Put mashed potatoes in pastry bag and pipe to make beard and brows, then shape potatoes into hat band and tassel. Put cherry-tomato nose in place. Cover hat with tomato paste. Arrange green-pepper leaves and tomatoes around Santa.

SHOWTIME

Gather guests around your tinfoil-covered uncooked Santa meatloaf and propose a toast: "Here comes Santa Claus!" Remove foil and reveal him raw. Allow selfie-with-Santa time. Re-cover with foil and bake in a 350-degree oven for 45 minutes. Remove foil and bake another 15 minutes until he is well done and looks delicious. Regather the group and pull him out of the oven. Slice and serve—hat first, beard next, face last, with plenty of garlic-parmesan cheese buns, butter, ketchup, and Christmas cheer!

NORTH WOODS INN

San Gabriel, CA

THE FAKE SNOW

on the roof is the crowning touch to the world's greatest log-cabin-lodge-themed restaurant. This over-the-top, high-cholesterol, high-altitude dining and drinking experiential extrava-ganza was lovingly handcrafted the old-fashioned way, log by log, in 1958. Inside, the décor is warm, rustic, and racy. Lighting is low with the glow of stained glass. Signs say THROW PEANUT SHELLS ON THE FLOOR. Old-school paintings of reclining nudes hang on the log walls, and the official greeter is a massive taxidermy bear. The menu is mainly meaty, but for me the main attractions are the bottomless red cabbage slaw, the blue cheese–smothered iceberg lettuce salad, and the famous, to-die-for cheese bread. Pioneers, prospectors, and fur trappers would feel right at home here.

SEEING SANTA

Some friends and I went to Knott's "Merry" Farm to enjoy the park all decked out for the holidays. Scampering around Ghost Town, we walked by the Santa meet 'n' greet. I suggested we go in and say hi to him, but we were stopped dead in our tracks by one of Santa's helpers, who was putting up a sign that said, "Santa will return in 30 minutes." Being grown-ups, we agreed that we really didn't need to see Santa, but secretly I still wanted to.

Later we happened by Santa's house again. This was our chance! As we walked up to the door, once again Santa's helper was putting out a sign that said, "Santa will return at 9 a.m." Now I *really* wanted to see Santa. Only Mrs. Knott's fried chicken could derail my disappointment. Too bad the line at the restaurant was out the door and we were too hungry to wait.

Off we went to the nearby North Woods Inn. We walked in and there he was: Santa! I thought I was dreaming. With no elves to stop us, we made a beeline for him. Barely containing my childlike excitement, I greeted him gleefully. He told us he had just finished at Knott's and wished us a Merry Christmas, adding, "No pictures, please!" I'm pretty sure he didn't want to be seen with the sexy blond he was sharing cheese bread with!

So finally, I got to see Santa! Life is full of surprises. Most of them are wonderful.

Warmth awaits you behind these wooden double doors with twin pines of stained glass.

The North Woods Inn was originally located in Monrovia, but was painstakingly moved, log by log, to San Gabriel when the new freeway was built in its path.

The North Woods Inn is a delightful place to enjoy dinner and drinks all year long, but especially at Christmastime!

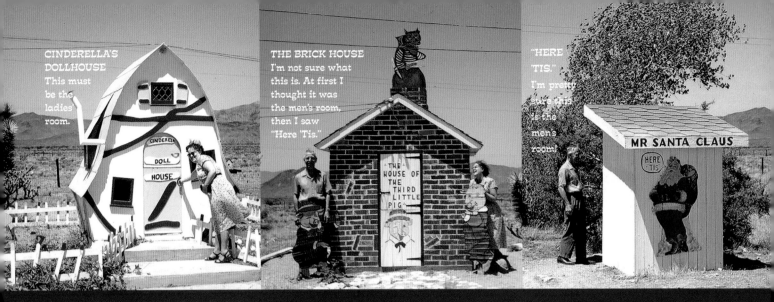

CINDERELLA'S DOLLHOUSE
This must be the ladies' room.

THE BRICK HOUSE
I'm not sure what this is. At first I thought it was the men's room, then I saw "Here 'Tis."

"HERE 'TIS."
I'm pretty sure this is the men's room!

THE HOUSE OF THE THIRD LITTLE PIG

MR SANTA CLAUS
HERE 'TIS

A FEW YEARS AGO, I was traveling across the desert on the old road between Las Vegas and Phoenix. I sped past a lone structure covered in graffiti. It seemed familiar, like I'd seen it before. I spun the car into a U-turn to investigate. As I pulled up, I realized I'd stumbled upon the landmark Christmas Tree Inn, in ruins and covered in layers of sunbaked spray paint.

In the late 1930s, Mr. and Mrs. Douglas opened a dining room catering to motorists passing through the desert. To attract more customers, they decorated the house for Christmas and changed the name to the Christmas Tree Inn. Dressed as Mr. and Mrs. Claus, they served a five-course meal of reindeer and chicken soup, Mary's Little Lamb Chops, North Pole Salad, and your choice of Stardust or Fairyland Cake for dessert. Ultimately their Christmas-themed restaurant inspired the name of the town: Santa Claus, AZ. By the 1970s the novelty had worn off and they stopped serving meals.

Not every Christmas story has a happy ending. But I was happy to discover this place, even covered in graffiti. I love to look through the layers of time.

CHRISTMAS TREE Inn

ENTRANCE

Greetings from SANTA CLAUS, ARIZONA
CHRISTMAS TREE INN
★ ★

"NO PARKING PLEASE" No problem, there's about a million other places to park the car! When I found these vintage slides, they were unmarked. I had no idea where this place was. Then I read the tailgate on the 1952 Pontiac station wagon, where it was spelled out for the world to see: Santa Claus, Arizona.

CHRISTMAS TREE INN

SANTA CLAUS, AZ, 1951

A 1950 Studebaker with its famous suicide doors is parked out front. Tourists pose with the patio furniture. A plywood Christmas tree is strung with lights, and a Santa cutout stands on the candy-cane-striped roof, ready to go down the chimney. Fine food is promoted in neon.

Lammes CANDIES

CHOCOLATE COVERED
STRAWBERRIES
APRIL 19 - 21

CANDIES Since 1885

There's no such thing as a trip to Austin, TX, without at least one sweet stop at LAMMES CANDIES, founded in the great Lone Star State in 1885. The colossal candy cane has been a landmark at the "new" location since 1956.

Jerry and Suzy Rowley and the "World's Largest Handmade Candy Cane." We made it for an extreme Christmas candy show on the Food Network. And yes, it's heavy!

CANDY CANE LANE

I can't imagine Christmas without Logan's candy canes. House-made the genuine, authentic, old-fashioned way, they've been a holiday tradition in my hometown of Ontario, CA, since 1933. Each one is spun-sugar perfection, looks like silk, and melts in your mouth. I've been east, west, north, and south and I've yet to find a better candy cane maker than Jerry Rowley. Throughout the year, he shares his sugar-spinning secrets, giving in-store candy cane and ribbon-candy-making demos, which always draw a crowd. Free warm samples, too. You can smell the sweetness a block away.

Candy Cane Motel

ANAHEIM, CA

Everyone gets a candy cane when they check in, just as they have since opening day on December 25, 1957.

ROCKEFELLER CENTER, NEW YORK, NY, 1959

Three candy canes, one mother, and a daughter with two heads—a festive family portrait photo-bombed by the most famous and photographed Christmas tree in the world, a holiday tradition since 1931. According to the legend, construction workers building the landmark art deco entertainment and office complex paid for and put up the first tree.

GET BUSY

Divide batter into two bowls and stir in peppermint extract to taste. Generously add red food coloring to one and white food coloring to the other. (Using red velvet cake batter WON'T do, it's simply not bright enough.) Fill plastic squeeze bottles with batter. Spray 3 cake pans with PAM. Line bottom of cake pans with no-stick baking paper. Flour sides of pans. To create the candy cane effect, squeeze in the red and white batter, alternating in concentric circles until pan is about 3/4 full. Bake cakes according to box instructions.

FROSTING and FILLING

Stir turquoise food coloring into frosting until color is consistent. Put several candy canes in a double-zip plastic bag and gently crack with a mallet until they are broken into small pieces and all your holiday aggressions are out. Sift to get rid of the teeny-tiny broken bits. Stack each layer with a generous spread of frosting sprinkled and topped with candy cane bits. Frost and refrigerate.

CRAZY CANDY CANE CAKE

3 boxes white cake mix, mixed according to box instructions

1 large bottle red food coloring

1 large bottle white food coloring

1 large bottle turquoise food coloring

Peppermint extract to taste

5 tubs white frosting

Small and large candy canes

Red, white, and green spice drops

Peppermint candies

SHOWTIME

To increase the chances that your candy cane cake will collapse during the party, decorate with candy canes, peppermints, amd spice drops just before your guests arrive. Let them oooh and aaah over it. Then let gravity do its thing—hopefully within an hour or so, much to their devilish delight, they'll witness the cake crack, fail, and fall. Serve the collapsed cake right away with holiday cheer and watch it get gobbled up like it was the last cake on the planet! By the way, it's totally fine if your crazy candy cane cake doesn't collapse—it'll still be the life of the party.

Candy Canes and Cake Collide in this Peppermint Party Pleaser!

Time to stock up on candy canes, bust out the red food coloring, and get your peppermint on!

This cake has an element of mystery to it. First, you have no idea how your candy cane batter is going to stripe when it bakes. Second, you have no idea if the cake will collapse—yes, collapse. Because of the extreme amount of candy canes stabbed into the top layer of this misfit mound of minty marvelousness, my cake developed several fault lines and within a couple of hours collapsed all over the table. But that was totally fine with me. What a memorable way to serve a cake!

It's Christmastime in the City

BRAND BOULEVARD, GLENDALE, CA, 1960
It's the magic midcentury hour. The street is sparkling with classic cars of the future and the warm, wondrous glow of neon. Swags and swirls of glittering garland span the street as far as the eye can see. High above it all, a stunning Christmas-light tree reigns supreme atop Glendale Federal Savings. Designed by master modernist architect W.A. Sarmiento in 1958, it's the most modern, up-to-date office building in town.

Let There Be Lights

A great way to start a new holiday tradition is to put Christmas lights on something iconic that's never been lit up before. Imagine the possibilities. I have a long to-light-up list but have only crossed off three so far.

☑ **THE BIG BOY**
The famous hamburger mascot at Bob's Big Boy Broiler in Downey, CA.

☑ **THE SPACE CAPSULE**
Columbia Memorial Space Center in Downey, CA.

☑ **WIGWAM** at the Wigwam Motel, a legendary Route 66 landmark n Rialto, CA, since 1950.

CHRISTMAS SHOPPING

J.W. Robinson's, PALM SPRINGS, CA, 1958
The timeless design and décor of this desert resort department store is the epitome of smart, sophisticated style. The fashions, fixtures, Christmas tree, and every other detail are exquisite in every way. Robinson's is long gone, but, thankfully, this building lives on as one of the many marvelous monuments that makes Palm Springs the mecca of midcentury modernism.

SEARS HAS YOU COVERED FOR CHRISTMAS. The iconic original big-box retailer has nearly everything you need to celebrate the season and then some. Shop till you drop-in store, or if you prefer to shop from the convenience of a catalog, no problem–Sears introduced its Christmas catalog in 1935 and called it the Wishbook. Paging through the Sears Christmas Wishbook is one of my earliest holiday memories. Every year when the coveted catalog arrived in the mail, my brother and I fought over who got to be the first one to go through it and circle all the toys we wanted. Then Christmas came, as did a few select toys and three new pairs of husky boy jeans.

When You Wish Upon a Sears

One Santa, two palms, three Christmas trees, eight reindeer, and a parking lot full of colorful cars. Welcome to Sears in Fresno, CA, dressed for the holidays, 1957.

The Cats' Pajamas
Even has "whiskers!"
Children's. State size 1, 2, 3, 4, 5, 6. Wt. 10 oz.
29 N 3254.........$2.83
Infants'. Gripper crotch.
State size small (to 12 mos., 22 lbs.); large (12 to 18 mos.; 22½ to 26 lbs.).
Shpg. wt. set 8 oz.
29 N 3253.........$2.83

MEOW
Leopard-print PJs are definitely the cat's pajamas in the 1959 Christmas catalog.

"OVER 40 STORES • EVERYTHING FOR EVERYBODY • PARKING FOR 6000 CARS"

Decades before STAR WARS was released in 1977, the Force was clearly with Shoppers' World. The ultra-modern, space-station-style strip mall, illustrated on the 1957 billboard (on the right) and pictured below at Christmas, is straight out of a sci-fi thriller, complete with zombie shoppers. The daring design of this double-decker, open-air shopping center was out of this world when it opened in 1951. A study in midcentury minimalism, it was a prototype for countless enclosed malls that followed. Jordan Marsh, the anchor tenant, was the only depart-ment store ever built in the round with a domed roof. Malls are like fashion—they go out of style, too. By the 1980s, Shoppers' World was yester-day's news, but managed to keep the doors open and lights on until 1993, when it was unceremoniously demolished to make way for an all-new "McMall."

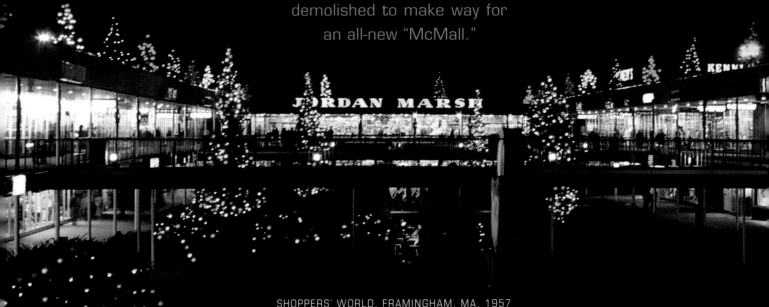

SHOPPERS' WORLD, FRAMINGHAM, MA, 1957

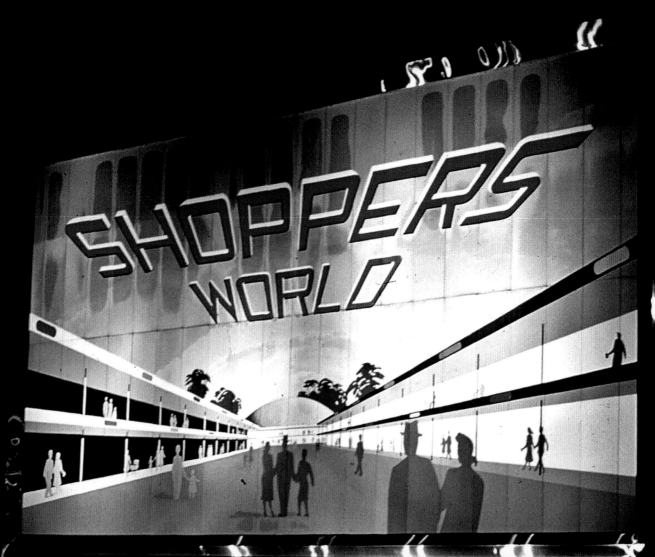

SHOPPERS WORLD

OVER 40 STORES · EVERYTHING FOR EVERYBODY · PARKING FOR 6000 CARS

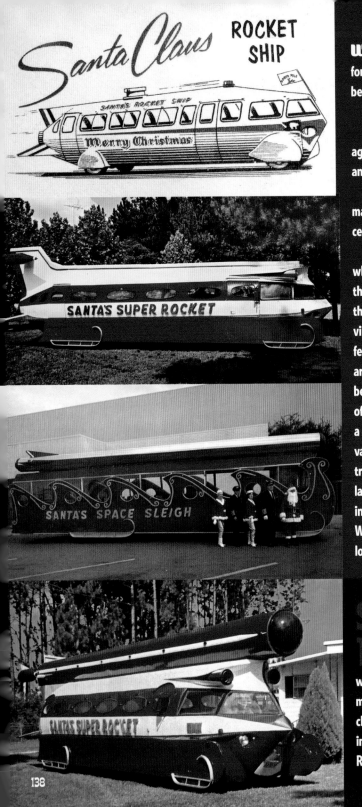

Santa Claus ROCKET SHIP

With the race for space in full swing in the late 1950s, former circus promoter Lloyd B. Laster of Tyler, TX, decided that Santa needed to be in tune with the times.

So he replaced Santa's iconic sleigh with a fleet of earth-bound rocket ships.

Over the next few years, Mr. Laster created four radical, custom-built, space-age-style vehicles. Each was well equipped with flashing lights and loudspeakers and staffed with a pilot, copilot, space hostess, and, of course, Santa.

The rockets toured Texas and the Midwest, appearing in holiday parades and making scheduled appearances at department stores, supermarkets, and shopping centers, where Santa welcomed children on board and took them for free rides.

When Mr. Laster retired in 1974, he sold the rockets to a man in Wisconsin who, according to legend, ran them there for a few more years. The evidence that these merry midcentury marvels even existed is sparse, to say the least. Besides these original promotional postcards, virtually no vintage color, and very few black and white, images are known to exist. What became of all but one of the rockets remains a mystery. Two vanished without a trace, while one was last seen in the '90s in a salvage yard in Wisconsin. Are they lost in space?

Santa's Moon Rocket

was the last addition to the fleet. He made a grand entrance in his kid-friendly meet 'n' greet home for the season. Parents could see and hear their child on closed-circuit TV talking to Santa inside his merry moon mobile after he arrived in his drivable (yes, drivable!) space capsule. Whatever became of Santa's Moon Rocket is a mystery.

Lost in Space

SANTA'S ROCKET SLEIGH

SANTA'S ROCKET SHIP

Lost & Found

This is the lucky one, the survivor. In the late '80s, MukLuk Land, a quirky roadside attraction in Tok, AK, purchased Santa's Rocket Ship, and that's where it survives and thrives to this day. It's a big hit every year in the annual Tok Christmas Parade.

SANTA'S ROCKET SHIP

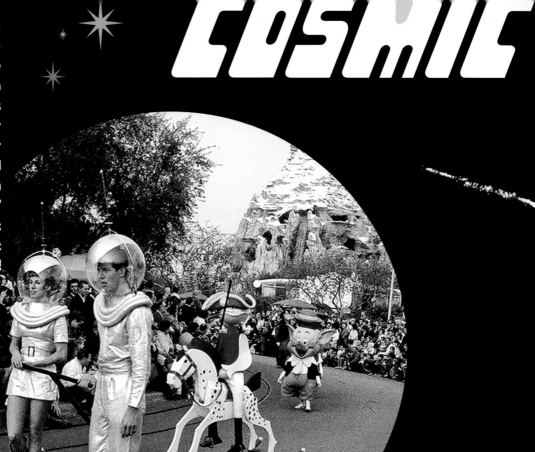

COSMIC

MR. AND MRS. TOMORROWLAND,
DISNEYLAND CHRISTMAS PARADE,
ANAHEIM, CA, 1966

With the legendary House of the Future and iconic Matterhorn as a dramatic backdrop, Tomorrowland's fab, futuristic duo are dressed for space-age success in matching silver spacesuits and bubbleheads wired with antennae. They live in a realm promoted as "the world of 1986." I remember 1986—I had an outfit just like that, only my skirt was shorter!

TINFOIL IN TINSELTOWN,
HOLLYWOOD'S 25TH ANNUAL SANTA CLAUS LANE PARADE, HOLLYWOOD, CA , 1953

I'm over the moon over SPACE PATROL's star-spangled and sparkling parade rocket, ready for takeoff. Aluminum foil has never been put to better use. SPACE PATROL was a popular 15-minute TV series that ran from 1950 to 1955. The show went into another dimension in 1953 when it became the first broadcast on television in 3-D.

CHRISTMAS

SPACE PATROL
KECA · TV ★ CHANNEL 7

I'VE NEVER MET A GINGERBREAD HOUSE I DIDN'T LIKE.
Whether they're miniature or massive, sloppy or spectacular, I love them all. When the day came for me to build one myself, I headed straight to Streit's German Bakery in Downey, CA, to seek the assistance of master gingerbread-house maker Oscar Streit. Under his watchful eye, I crafted a sweet little A-frame sugar shack. I kept it small because all along my plan was to blast it off to outer space. When I told Oscar that this gingerbread house would go where no gingerbread house had ever gone before, he very sternly stated…

"GINGERBREAD HOUSES DON'T FLY!

FOR THE BLASTOFF, I brought my finished gingerbread house to "the Cradle of the Cosmic Age," the former site of Northrup, also in Downey. Since all six of the command modules that took man to and from the moon were designed and built there, it seemed like the perfect place to launch my little gingerbread house into the stratosphere.

I met up with "ballusionist" Brian Potvin. We attached helium-filled balloons to the base of the house. By the time we were ready for flight, a curious crowd had gathered.

With a spirited "5-4-3-2-1 BLASTOFF!" we launched the little dead-weight dough domicile into the wild blue yonder. As it lifted off for outer space, everyone cheered. Brian and I jumped up and down screaming, "We did it, we did it!"

In a matter of mere moments, the cheers turned into loud gasps and cries of horror. I looked up. I saw the balloons but no house. Oscar was right: "Gingerbread houses don't fly!"

SPLAT!

Season's Greetings

Hallmark is a pillar of civilization: an iconic, creative, cultural, and social institution that knows no equal.

the four of us are wishing you

THE UNSUNG HERO of occasional and seasonal sociology is J.C. Hall, who didn't invent the greeting card but certainly perfected it. In 1910, at the age of 18, he began printing greetings on postcards in Kansas City, MO. Two Christmases later, his first holiday cards were a big hit. In 1915, for the sake of his customers' privacy, he revolutionized printed greetings when he introduced the folded card and included an envelope with purchase. Hall was on a roll. And so was his wrapping paper. In 1917, he was the first to offer decorative gift wrap that was precut and rolled.

By the 1920s, with a dizzying nationwide distribution network of dazzling displays in drugstores and stationery shops, the Hallmark brand had cozied up with the masses and was well established as the "it" greeting card and decorative-paper company.

In 1944, the brilliant, long-surviving advertising slogan, "When You Care Enough to Send the Very Best," was coined by a smart salesman. Hallmark's crowning touch, its timeless logo that epitomizes what I call a "font of optimism," first graced the back of a card in 1949.

The next year, the colossal card company opened its first modern brick-and-mortar store. From there, the empire snowballed into a coast-to-coast chain of retail Hallmark Shops brimming with its ever-evolving collections of cards, gifts, and seasonal décor.

Today, Hallmark is the oldest and grandest greeting card company in the United States. After all it's done, the immeasurable amount of gracious goodwill and kind wishes it has spread, I think we should send Hallmark a thank-you card. And when we do, of course it will be a Hallmark card, because it deserves to receive the very best!

Ready-to-Tear

Joining the short-lived paper-dress fad in the late 1960s, Hallmark made the leap into single-use fashions. Unlike other paper-dress manufacturers, Hallmark offered a complete collection of matching plates, napkins, and party products.

Merry
MIDCENTURY
Modern

We're looking through the sliding glass doors, the most exciting feature of every suburban midcentury Southern California tract home. The lights are on, everyone is home, and the room is all aglow with honey-blond and sage-green warmth. Everybody and everything is in its perfect place around the tree, even the weenie dog. Colorful Christmas cards hang like modern art on the wall. Gift boxes are neatly stacked tree-side. Even the copper canisters in the kitchen are in line. Junior is looking at us with that "pride-of-new-toy-car-ownership" expression. All other eyes are on Daddy-O... he has a rifle!
Merry Christmas!

INDIO, CA, 1957

I Wish You a Merry

TOILET PAPER TREE

PALM FROND TREE

FISHNET TREE

ORIGAMI TREE

Christmas Tree

TWISTED TREE

UMBRELLA TREE

The Christmas Tree is the ultimate gathering place, gift hub, and centerpiece of the season. Public and private, live and fake, forest grown and factory made, they appear in many styles, shapes, and sizes. I think decorating and displaying a tree is an underrated form of expression. It doesn't matter how many decorations your tree has or doesn't have, or whether it is flocked, floating, or flaming. What matters is that your tree has heart and soul.

The Life of a Real Christmas Tree

We hunt down the prettiest pine, cram it in the car, drag it into the house, electrify it with lights, drown it with decorations, and then spend the next couple of weeks admiring it as it cooks, wilts, and dies. When the party is over, out on the curb it goes, waiting to be eaten by the garbage truck and spit out at the dump. Ironically, if you want to go green, get a fake tree...

...and then there's no need to get Christmas tree sap and pine needles all over the backseat of your brand-new 1957 Fairlane 500 Sunliner convertible.

149

LIGHT-UP JELL-O CHRISTMAS TREE

Jell-O is in a culinary class all its own. It comes in a complete rainbow of artificial colors and fake flavors. It'll even dance for you. Since the ultimate "just-add-water" wonder-of-the-world was first introduced in the late 1890s, countless molded concoctions, both sweet and savory, have been the super-star spectacles of many a luncheon, dinner, and dessert table. The Jell-O Museum, in Leroy, NY, is housed in the historic building where this gelatinous joy was mass-produced between 1900 and 1964.

PLUG IT IN, IT LIGHTS UP ...AND COULD KILL YOU!

"WILL I GET ELECTROCUTED IF I PUT TWINKLE LIGHTS IN JELL-O?" EVERY ELECTRICIAN I ASKED SAID, "YES."

I decided to do it anyway. To see Jell-O twinkle from within, I was willing to die. I don't call it the "Test Kitchen" for nothing.

For this jolly Jell-O mold, only a traffic cone would do.

In need of Jell-O expertise for this potentially fatal project, I met up with Michelle Quiles, owner of Blooming Gelatin Art in East Los Angeles. When the tree was ready to be lit, we held our breath, and, with a nervous "5-4-3-2-1," I plugged it in.

The sight of sparkling Jell-O was electrifying. I wasn't sure if I was dead or alive, but I was certain this was the most joyful Jell-O moment of my life.

GET BUSY

In a large pot, prepare Jell-O and Knox gelatin in just enough water to fit in traffic cone. Add food coloring. Wrap Styrofoam cone with foil. Attach twinkle lights around Styrofoam cone, using bobby pins to keep them in place. Leave plug sticking out at bottom. Seal the top of traffic cone with a drain stopper. Spray inside of cone with cooking spray. Place twinkle light–wrapped Styrofoam cone into traffic cone. Pour lime Jell-O liquid mix to the brim. Refrigerate for 12 hours to do what Jell-O does: gel. When well-gelled, remove from fridge and turn over onto sturdy platter. To de-cone, get out your blow dryer and heat cone just enough to release your Light-Up Jell-O Christmas Tree. Phew, you did it!

Have a **LIGHT-UP JELL-O CHRISTMAS TREE** contest party. Extra points if it spins and has a music box in it!

GET THIS

3 boxes lime Jell-O
10 packets Knox gelatin
1 small bottle green food coloring
18-inch Styrofoam cone
Extra-wide aluminum foil
3 strands Christmas twinkle lights
Clean, unused 24-inch traffic cone
Drain stopper

SHOWTIME

Display your about-to-be-electrified Jell-O creation for all the world to see. When the moment is just right, gather the gang around, hold up the cord, have 911 on speed dial, and on the count of 5-4-3-2-1...plug in that Jell-O, and be glad to be alive!

WONDER WHEEL

Motorized Multicolor
Midcentury
Marvelousness

What butter is to bread and Ethel is to Lucy, the COLOR WHEEL is to the aluminum Christmas tree. As if Christmas wasn't already colorful enough, the kitschy kaleidoscope was born to be the shining, spinning sidekick of the space-age spruce. They're a perfect pair and a sparkling success. Extra points if your aluminum Christmas tree is in a rotating stand. Then they'll both be spinning, and so will your head, exploding with seasonal sensationalism and joy overload! And who said color wheels are for Christmas only? They can survive without their tinsel tree to shine on. I should know, because I keep my color wheel spinning nightly all year long. Life in my living room wouldn't be the same without it.

CHRISTMAS OFFICIALLY ENTERED THE AGE OF SPACE IN 1959 when the Aluminum Specialty Company of Manitowoc, WI, introduced the "Evergleam" aluminum Christmas tree. The small town, promoted as the "Aluminum Cookware Capital of the World," was the leading manufacturer of coffee percolators, electric frying pans, and Jell-O molds. Who knew that aluminum Christmas trees and Jell-O molds are cousins?

The genius idea to mass-produce aluminum Christmas trees came from the company's sales manager in 1958, after he spotted handmade silver tinsel trees in a holiday display window of a Chicago department store.

The Evergleam Trees were an instant sensation. Dozens of other manufacturers followed suit, and hundreds of thousands were produced, enough to fill a foil forest.

Silver not good enough for you? No problem—the sparkly spruces were also made, though in far fewer numbers, in pink, green, turquoise, gold, and black. By the end of the 1960s, the tinfoil-tree craze began to tarnish. The Aluminum Specialty Company harvested its last crop in 1971. Today these metallic midcentury marvels are prized collectibles, the very definition of classic Christmas kitsch.

SPACE-AGE SPRUCE

ASTRO-WEENIE CHRISTMAS TREE

The ASTRO-WEENIE CHRISTMAS TREE transcends class. You can take one to your kid's nursery school or present one to the Queen of England! Show up with one at a holiday party and you're the belle of the ball. Your ASTRO-WEENIE CHRISTMAS TREE can be sweet or savory or both. And just about anything you can stick a toothpick through will do, as long as it's edible. Be creative and don't forget the most important ingredient of all: cocktail weenies!

GET THIS

- 24-inch Styrofoam cone
- Extra-wide tinfoil
- Straight pins
- 2 tbsps. peanut butter
- 2 packs cocktail weenies
- 1 box multicolored toothpicks

MIX & MINGLE

ANY OR ALL OF THE FOLLOWING WILL DO:

- Pickles
- Olives
- Baby corn
- Maraschino cherries
- Carrot sticks
- Celery sticks
- Cauliflower
- Broccoli
- Radishes
- Grapes
- Kumquats
- Crab apples
- Donut holes
- Peeled shrimp
- Cheese chunks
- Cheeto balls
- Gummy bears
- Cherry tomatoes
- Swedish meatballs
- Pineapple chunks
- Star fruit

GET BUSY

Cover Styrofoam cone with foil. Use pins to keep it in place.

Smear the bare bottom of the Styrofoam cone with peanut butter to "glue" it to the plate.

Fry cocktail weenies until they are golden brown and perfuming the whole house with their intoxicating smell. Sample a few to make sure they're just right.

Make sure the pineapple or anything else out of a can or jar is well drained OVERNIGHT before putting it on the tree. Nobody wants a drippy tree. Brighten up well-drained canned pineapple by tossing in a few drops of yellow food coloring.

Spike the fruits, veggies, and wonderful weenies with multicolored toothpicks and stick them into the Styrofoam with force. Wear a thimble, otherwise the sharp toothpicks will prick your tender little fingers.

For the crowning touch, if you can't find a star fruit for the topper, no problem—a yellow bell pepper or thick slice of cheddar cheese cut into a star shape will shine just as brightly!

If you have pyro tendencies and want your ASTRO-WEENIE TREE ON FIRE, simply stick birthday candles into the weenies. Have a friend or two help you light them just before presentation.

Have an ASTRO-WEENIE CHRISTMAS TREE CONTEST PARTY! What's better than one Astro-Weenie Christmas Tree? A whole forest of them!

SHOWTIME

Serve it surrounded with your favorite dips and dressings centered on the most prominent table in the house.

THERE ARE TWO KINDS OF CHRISTMAS TREE LOTS: those that flock and those that don't. When given the choice, we prefer those that flock. They are called flock lots.

GET FLOCKED!

THE TRADITION IN MY FAMILY was that we always got our Christmas tree on my birthday—December 20th—and I got to pick it out. When I was in first grade, I chose a white flocked tree. It was the best Christmas tree we ever had. We didn't put lights on it because my worrywart mother was afraid it would catch on fire and burn the whole house down. We never got a flocked tree again.

Last Christmas, I decided that after all these years, I was finally going to get another flocked tree. Not an ordinary white one—been there, done that! No, I wanted a tree flocked in a bright color, like turquoise or pink.

By chance I happened upon a flock lot. I almost crashed the car as my head exploded over the intoxicating display of trees in more flocking colors than I'd ever seen before: pink, purple, blue, green, yellow, and orange. Drunk with pleasure and feeling the seasonal spirit like never before, I wasted no time finding the flocker to shower him with compliments. He told me he'd been flocking professionally for 35 years. I just about melted when he said he'd flock a tree especially for me.

But then came the monumental decision: What color? I love them all. I couldn't decide. "Surprise me!" When I went back to pick up the tree, I couldn't believe my eyes—I got *all* the colors! He flocked me the rainbow Christmas tree that I'd been dreaming of all along.

Life is full of surprises, most of them wonderful, but few as colorful as this one.

Rarely do we do the flocking ourselves. We let someone else flock for us.

But for those who want to flock themselves, you can flock yourself at home!

FLOCK LOT
WILSHIRE BLVD., LOS ANGELES, 1957

157

SPINNING or FLOATING?
How to set your tree adrift, atwirl, or both!

Merry Go Round

Part tree spinner and part tree uplight, the vintage Lorelei revolving tree stand is all that and much more. It's also part music box, with its very own holiday playlist to serenade you with just a flip of a foot switch.

Go Float Your Tree

THANKS TO FLOATING CHRISTMAS TREE MASTERMIND JEFF NEPPL FOR SHOWING US HOW IT'S DONE!

GET THIS

- 36-INCH PLYWOOD DISC
- STURDY TREE STAND
- 4 36-INCH-LONG ZIP TIES
- 36-INCH INNER TUBE
- CHRISTMAS TREE
- SEVERAL STRINGS OF LIGHTS
- DECORATIONS
- 60-INCH TREE SKIRT
- SWIMMING POOL
- ROPE

GET BUSY

Drill four 1-inch holes evenly spaced on plywood disc, 3 inches from edge. Bolt tree stand to center of disc. Thread zip ties through holes and around inner tube to attach inner tube to disc. Place tree in stand and secure. String lights, decorate tree, and dress with tree skirt. Float tree in pool, being sure to tether to the edge with rope. Stand back in awe of what you've created.

SHOWTIME

Proudly gather guests around the pool, light the lights, propose a toast, say "Cheers," untether the tree, and give it a hearty push-off. All will be floored as it floats around your pretty pool like it's waltzing.

Denver, CO, 1955

TOO MUCH IS NEVER ENOUGH

The photographer marked this slide: "Mr. and Mrs. Gano Senter's famous Christmas tree. 4,000 ornaments, 1,000 lights, 350 birds–16 trees to make this one." With this info I went online to find out more about this "famous Christmas tree." What I found was a lot more than I bargained for. Go ahead and Google, but be forewarned, the Senters were more naughty than nice, to say the least.

You'll have to turn off the Christmas lights to see the radiant aura of Shiny Brite's Glo in the Dark ornaments.

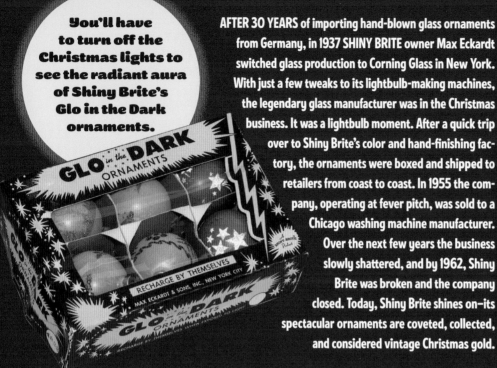

AFTER 30 YEARS of importing hand-blown glass ornaments from Germany, in 1937 SHINY BRITE owner Max Eckardt switched glass production to Corning Glass in New York. With just a few tweaks to its lightbulb-making machines, the legendary glass manufacturer was in the Christmas business. It was a lightbulb moment. After a quick trip over to Shiny Brite's color and hand-finishing factory, the ornaments were boxed and shipped to retailers from coast to coast. In 1955 the company, operating at fever pitch, was sold to a Chicago washing machine manufacturer. Over the next few years the business slowly shattered, and by 1962, Shiny Brite was broken and the company closed. Today, Shiny Brite shines on—its spectacular ornaments are coveted, collected, and considered vintage Christmas gold.

GREAT BALLS of CHRISTMAS

Keeping up with the space-age style of the day, Bubble Lites blasted off with rocket-shaped bases in the early '60s.

WATCH THEM BUBBLE

8-LIGHT SERIES SET

NOMA BUBBLE LITES

BUBBLE UP

BUBBLE LITES are the ultimate in Christmas tree illumination. The intoxicating sparklers were a smash hit when introduced by Noma, of Glenview, IL, in 1946. The company claimed that the lights would bubble for 1,000 hours, and that if they occasionally became lazy, they could be reactivated with the flick of a fingertip. The heat of the little lightbulb causes the wonder liquid inside to boil. If one seeps, leaks, or breaks, evacuate the area immediately—boiling Bubble Lites can be toxic.

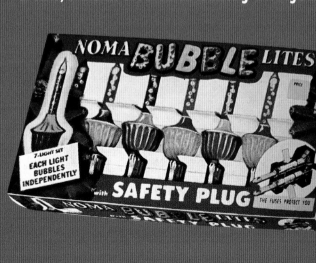

NOMA BUBBLE LITES

7-LIGHT SET
EACH LIGHT BUBBLES INDEPENDENTLY

with SAFETY PLUG

THE FUSES PROTECT YOU

Christmas Treehouse

Are your living room shelves full? No problem. Put the Nativity in the tree!

Troll Power

Trolls reign supreme in this living room, where apparently, there is only one place left for the nativity, shoved in the fireplace!

NATIVITY NOVELTIES

Drive-Thru Nativity

Car culture meets Christ in the parking lot of the First Christian Church in Huntington Beach, CA. Actors with live animals tell the story just as they have annually since 1968. I was blessed to experience this seasonal spectacle while sitting in the front seat of a 1955 Buick Roadmaster. Honk if you love Jesus!

The Nativity becomes the MEATivity

in this jaw-dropping, edible, holy holiday appetizer platter of delectable deli meats, hot dogs, ham, bacon, ground sirloin, sausage, and salami. The Wise Men bear the perfect gift for the little cocktail-weenie baby: Marbits from Lucky Charms. They're magically delicious!

GET THIS

1 bag frozen hash browns	Skewers & toothpicks
1 package hot dogs	1 lb. ground sirloin
1 package bologna	1 package foot-long hot dogs
1 package sliced salami	4 pretzel sticks
1 package ham lunchmeat	3 Lucky Charms Marbits

GET BUSY

Cover baking sheet with foil and spread with frozen hash browns. To make Wise Men, dress regular hot dogs in lunchmeat and bacon, using toothpicks to hold in place. Finish with Lucky Charms "gifts." Sculpt ground meat for manger animals. Insert pretzels for horns. To make the stable, skewer and toothpick regular and foot-long hot dogs notched like Lincoln Logs. Drape bacon for rooftop. Finish with a yellow toothpick star. If you can't figure out hot dog architecture, call an architect.

SHOWTIME

Proudly display your Meativity raw for all your guests to delightfully discover as they arrive. When everyone is present and has a drink in hand, hold up your meaty masterpiece, propose a toast to the newborn hot dog king, and throw the whole thing in a 325° oven. Thirty minutes later, gather guests around your oven and pull out the deliciously done Meativity. There will be gasps! Serve with warm, toasted buttered buns, hot mustard, and plenty of beer. Praise be!

the Meativity

This Gives
"Meet the Newborn King"
a Whole New Meaning!

163

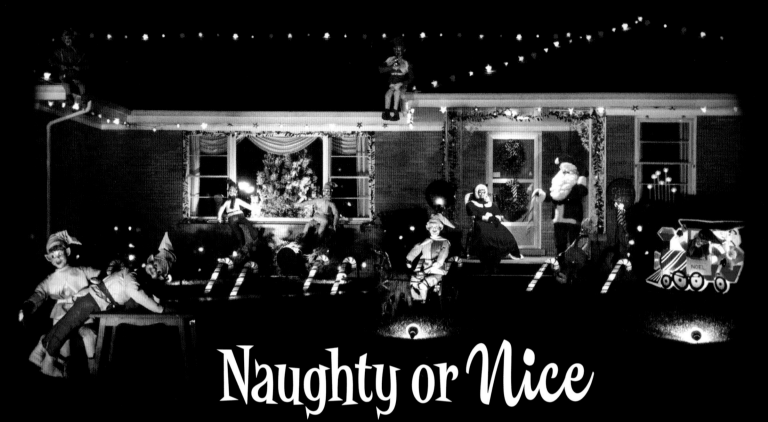

Naughty or Nice

Homeowners express themselves in many ways, but none are quite as revealing as the way they decorate their yards at Christmastime.

You Better Watch Out

All eyes are on the spanker and the spankee. Santa and Mrs. Claus and five fellow elves are transfixed. They don't want to miss a beat. And yes, you can watch too. The head of holiday display at this house is clearly feeling a little more than just the spirit of the season. This gives "naughty or nice" a whole new meaning. Bend over, it's Christmas!

Be Good for Goodness Sake

"For unto us a child is born" is written across a pink foil-covered, two-car garage door like your grandmother's handwriting on a billboard. The picture window frames a tri-tone trio of flocked trees. At the front door is a walk-through bell complete with a dong that's big enough to sit on and swing into the house. This gives doorbell a whole new meaning. Ding Dong!

Silent Night

Not sure what these 1950s caroling clones are singing, because we can't hear them. Their song is silent. These pretty people are blow molds, born of plastic at Mold-Craft Inc. of Port Washington, WI. The kid, straddling a mini pine tree, gives O Holy Night a whole new meaning. Even the dog thinks it's weird!

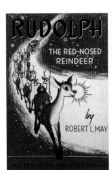

RUDOLPH
the RED-NOSED
REINDEER

The legend of the most famous reindeer of all, as the song rightfully claims, first appeared in a 1939 booklet by Robert L. May, published by the Montgomery Ward department store of Chicago. In 1949, the story was set to a memorable melody and recorded by cowboy star Gene Autry. Rudolf went down in history, becoming one of the top-selling singles of all time.

I'll Be Mobile Home for Christmas

The words MOBILE and HOME came together in 1956, when the first ten-foot-wide trailer was manufactured. This pretty, pink-trimmed, long, long trailer is ready for takeoff. The carport canopy and patio cover are spread like wings. Imagine harnessing up that cute little herd of blow-up plastic red-nosed reindeer and setting sail across the sky, just like Santa. Or better yet, imagine firing up that glistening gold 1957 Plymouth Belvedere, backing it out, hitching it up, and flooring it. You'd be flying in no time!

SNOW JOB

DOWNEY, CA, 1964

By any snowfall standards, this was quite a storm. Even the twin TV antennae are covered. It's freezing, too—icicles are hanging from the eaves. Just kidding! It's not cold; the icicles are tinfoil, and the snow is faux. While others in SoCal were dreaming about a white Christmas, the Miller family, standing ankle deep in it, made it happen. Imagine how lucky you'd have been to live across the street from this wannabe winter wonderland. Every morning during the holiday season, you could've peered through your big picture window and wondered why there were no birds left in the neighborhood. If the melt-proof snowman's friendly smile didn't attract your attention, his flailing motorized arms would have. Yep, he's animated!

167

FROSTY
the
CHEESE
BALL
MAN

Plug Him
In and He
Melts

Into
Cheezy
Dip!

168

Velveeta

has always fascinated me. I love saying VEL-VEEE-TUH as much as I secretly love eating it: melted, of course. The idea for melting a snowman made of Velveeta balls covered in cream cheese came to me as an epiphany while driving from Seattle to Portland. It hit me like a ton of Velveeta bricks. As soon as I got home, I was crafting the first Frosty the Cheese Ball Man. He landed in my favorite vintage flying saucer-shaped electric skillet and performed right on cue by melting into queso before he could even say, "I'll be back again someday."

get this

2 32-oz blocks
  Velveeta
3 8-oz bricks
  cream cheese
1 green bell pepper
1 red bell pepper
1 carrot
2 slices black olive
2 pretzel sticks
Electric skillet

get busy

Hand roll room-temperature Velveeta into three beautiful balls: small, medium, and large. Frost each with cream cheese as smoothly as you can. Stack the balls, centered, in an unplugged electric skillet. Get creative with the veggies, dressing him well and bringing him to life with a happy face.

showtime

Have Frosty prominently placed so your guests can't miss him when they arrive. After everyone has been served a cocktail, gather them around the cheerful cheese ball stack and propose a hearty toast: "Here's to and cheers to Frosty the Cheese Ball Man!" Plug in the skillet and set the dial to 350 degrees. For the next 30 minutes, watch in shock and awe as he slowly melts into an addictive cheezy dip! Careful that he doesn't get too hot—you want Frosty melted, not burned! Serve with your favorite chips or whatever else you like dipped into a melted meld of Velveeta and cream cheese.

GO GLAM!

Cheers to the lady in the timeless-classic ostrich feather hat. Cheers to the Hugh Hefner wannabe. Cheers to those shocking pink toreador/pedal pusher/clamdigger/capri hostess pants. And double cheers to her bullet brassiere.

What to Wear

Your Guide to Fun, Festive Fashions

Go Christmas Tree!

Go Tree Skirt!

Go Pixie!

Go Pinocchio!

Go Cops & Robbers!

Go Flaming!

Go Tiger!

Go Field & Stream!

WHEN I WAS ASKED TO PERFORM

my Retro Holiday Show at Modernica Props, located in Los Angeles's former Twinkie and Ho Ho factory (really), my brain almost exploded whipped cream! The mere thought of being on the site where zillions of Hostess's most famous snack treats had raced around on conveyor belts for decades intoxicated me into a state of divine culinary creativity. That's when Twink & Ho was born. This is sweet deliciousness and decadence like your tongue has never tasted before.

GET THIS

Large punch bowl

4 packages instant vanilla pudding, mixed according to box instructions

Peppermint extract to taste

1 small bottle red food coloring

1 small bottle green food coloring

1 large bag peppermint candies

4 large tubs Cool Whip

30 Twinkies

30 Ho Hos

2 dozen each large and small candy canes

1 jar maraschino cherries

GET BUSY

PREP THE PUDDING: Divide pudding into two bowls. Add mint extract to taste. Generously add red food coloring to one and green to the other.

SMASHING CANDY: Put some peppermint candies into a double zip-lock bag and tap lightly with a hammer until they are broken into small pieces. Sift to get rid of the really teeny broken bits.

LAYERING: Cover bottom of punch bowl with 1 inch of red pudding. Place a ring of Twinkies around the bowl so the bottom sides of Twinkies face outward. Fill in the middle with broken Twinkies. Cover with Cool Whip and sprinkle with crushed peppermints. Layer with half of green pudding, half of Ho Hos, and crushed peppermints. Repeat each layer. Finish with layer of Cool Whip and decorate with a colorful kaleidoscope of Christmas candy and cherries. If you have leftover Twinkies or Ho Hos, eat them before someone else does.

SHOWTIME

Gather everyone around, take time for a Twink & Ho group shot, and then serve it gleefully, grinning from ear to ear. Be prepared for your party peeps to gobble it all up. By the end of the night they'll be licking the bowl and begging for more.

TWINK & HO

Luscious Layered Peppermint Party Pudding

STEP CHILDREN
This really would be the picture-perfect family portrait—except they don't look a thing alike!

CLOWNING AROUND THE CHRISTMAS TREE
Party balloons make great Christmas tree ornaments!

BRICKS AND MORTAR
Of all the uses for cardboard, none are better to me than a fake fireplace. As a kid, I begged my parents for one, but the answer was always, "No, we have a real one." I would've preferred a fake one.

BY THE CHIMNEY WITH CARE: ANATOMY OF A CHRISTMAS STOCKING
A ball, a top, a Hansel and Gretel storybook, Colonial logs, gems and minerals, a guitar-playing doll, and fun toys. Judging by the contents, this stocking goes both ways...it's bisoxual!

pajama party

Traditionally, PJs are the one and only gift that kids are allowed to open on Christmas Eve.

Be a Christmas Clown

Dressing the kids in matching pajamas for a Christmas Eve portrait is normal. Matching clown pajamas are not. Especially with clown hand puppets to match. The show starts at midnight!

MIAMI BEACH, FL, 1959

It's a Wrap

The reason for the season and the ultimate holiday tradition is the gift exchange. The custom of Christmas gift giving began ages before merchants spun it into an unavoidable shopping spree and exhausting exercise of abundance. The art and craft of concealing the identify of a gift for maximum surprise requires creative cutting, folding, taping, and bow-tying skills. Wrapping is as much of a Christmas custom as the gifts themselves.

Killer Christmas
I'm not sure what's in the big box, but I am sure what's on it: a very nicely knotted noose!

Fit to Be Tied
You're a gift, so show up for Christmas dressed like one!

Don't Box Me In
This is the gift that grew in the box after it was wrapped.

177

I LOVE LUCY FAN

BEST FRIEND

MOTHER

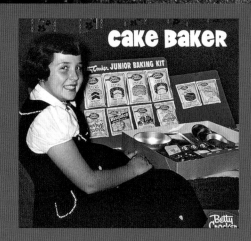

CAKE BAKER

PATTY PLAYPAL, a plastic wannabe three-year-old, is dressed for success in a party dress, socks, underwear, and black patent leather shoes. The Ideal Toy Company, famous for inventing the teddy bear in 1903, cloned countless copies of Patty beginning in 1959. And yes, there was a Peter Playpal!

PRETTY WOMAN

Lionel Trains, founded in New York City in 1900, was the ultimate go-to for model train sets. In 1957, it introduced a pastel-colored set targeted at girls. Too bad it flopped. Toy stores sold the unsold sets back to Lionel, which repainted and resold them as boys' toys.

TRAIN CONDUCTOR

NURSE

TELEPHONE OPERATOR

ENTREPRENEUR

GIRLS' GIFTS

When I grow up, I wanna be a...

ZOOKEEPER

HAPPY HOMEMAKER

HOME WRECKER

PRO SURFER

PRO SKIER

U.S. MARSHAL

FARMER

BOYS' TOYS

When I grow up, I wanna be a...

COWBOY

SPORTY SHERIFF

COUNTRY SQUIRE

PREACHER

HIGHWAY PATROLMAN

JACK OF ALL TRADES

ALIEN MONSTER

COMPUTER PROGRAMMER

SAD CLOWN

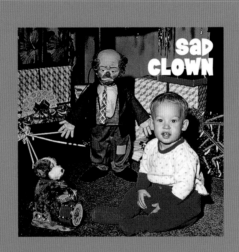

GAS STATION ATTENDANT

THE GREAT GARLOO

Made by Marx Toys of New York City, the battery-operated, remote-control, "unchained, unconquerable sci-fi movie monster" debuted in 1961. He moves back and forth, bends over, and picks up objects. Nice leopard-print boxers, too!

MILTON
BRADLEY

is the grand-
daddy of board
games. Begin-
ning in 1860, in
Springfield, MA,
he invented the
industry of pop-
ular games. Lest
they be confused
with gambling,
his games were
often played
with spinners
instead of dice.

182

GAMES PEOPLE PLAY

The Twist was in full swing in 1966 when Twister was introduced, and it became an instant sensation. The game board was super-sized in plastic and put on the floor, and players became the game pieces. It was the perfect game at the perfect time.

SHENANIGANS

CANDY LAND
Game

OPERATION
SKILL GAME
WHERE YOU'RE
THE DOCTOR

CHRISTMAS ISN'T CHRISTMAS WITHOUT A NEW BOARD GAME UNDER THE TREE!

SHENANIGANS,
the "Carnival of Fun" game, was based on a children's game show that aired during the 1964-65 season.

CANDY LAND
was created in 1949 by a polio patient in San Diego, CA, for fellow patients to enjoy while convalescing.

OPERATION,
introduced in 1965, was invented by a University of Illinois industrial design student.

GOING PLACES

There is no better Christmas gift for a kid than wheels. Bicycles, tricycles, and pedal cars promise mobility, independence, adventure, and speed.

183

HIS 'n HERS Gift GUIDE

for him...
a bare rug and
a bare ass!

What They Really Want

for her...
a bottle of booze and a
mirror, so she can get drunk,
hold up the mirror, and tell herself how pretty she is!

for her... MIDCENTURY MINK

Short of gems and jewels, a fur coat was the most desired gift for a man to give his wife or girlfriend. If you can't afford a real fur, give her a fake and hope she doesn't know the difference!

REAL MINK COAT

FAKE MINK STOLE

THE BEST GIFTS

for him... A BRAND-NEW CAR-TRUCK

Few things are more important to a man than his wheels. When you can't decide whether to give him a car or a truck, give him both... THE ALL-NEW-FOR-1967 RANCHERO BY FORD!

Gifts Not to Give
What they really don't want...

Household Appliances

Yard Equipment

Toilet Seats

CHERPUMPLE

Three pies baked into a three-layer cake

I dare you to try this at home. Cherpumple is **CHER**ry pie in white cake, **PUMP**kin in yellow, and app**LE** in spice, stacked and slathered with loads of cream cheese frosting. It's the most talked-about decadent dessert to come along in decades.

Cherpumple Saves the Planet

It was a typical family holiday at my aunt's house. The usual cast of related characters were there. We'd finished dinner and dessert, and a teetering tower of paper plates was stacked in the garbage.

That prompted me to call an emergency family meeting. I said, "Look at all those paper plates we're wasting, with everybody grazing and having 'just a sliver' of each of the several desserts on separate plates! We need to be a green family. Next year I'm going to bake all our desserts together, and everyone just gets one paper plate!"

I kept my promise. The very next year, I baked the pumpkin and apple pies into layers of our traditional Christmas cake, which has one yellow layer and one spice layer. For extra height, heft, and flavor, I added a third layer—a cherry pie baked into white cake. When the three pies stuffed into three cakes were stacked and smothered in cream cheese frosting, it was a bright beacon of light, practically too heavy to lift. The Cherpumple was born! And so was a new family tradition. Everyone gobbled it up, we saved paper plates, and we're now officially a green family.

Making a Cherpumple takes over your life for three days.

DAY 1 * Bake the pies.

DAY 2 * Bake pies in cake.

DAY 3 * Stack, frost, serve, and shine!

The Ultimate Holiday Dessert

GET THIS

3 8-inch frozen Sara Lee pies:
cherry, pumpkin, and apple

*

1 box each
spice, yellow, and white
cake mix, mixed according
to box instructions

*

3 10-inch cake pans

*

PAM

*

6 tubs cream cheese
frosting

GET BUSY

Bake Pies

Don't burn the pies, but bake them according to box instructions until well done. Cool to room temperature overnight to firm them up and prepare them to be stuffed inside a layer of cake and baked again. The pies have absolutely NO idea they're getting baked twice, so don't worry about it. Whatever you do, DO NOT REFRIGERATE PIES after baking.

How to Stuff a

1 Spray cake pans with PAM and line bottoms with rounds of no-stick paper. Flour sides of pans. For each of the 3 cakes, pour 1 inch batter in pan.

2 With a baked pie in one hand and a sturdy plate in the other, gently place the plate on top of the pie and quickly flip over.

3 Carefully remove the tin from the pie. Try your best not to crack the pie—they're fragile, and the crust tends to stick to the tin. I "twist" the tin off the bottom of the pie.

Pie in a Cake... It's as Easy as Pie!

4 With the de-tinned pie now upside down on the plate in one hand, put another plate over the pie and quickly flip it over.

5 Now you have a face-up, de-tinned pie on a plate. You're almost there.

6 Place the pie on the plate directly over the batter in the cake pan.

7 Gently but quickly, take a deep breath, channel your inner magician, and smoothly slide the pie into the batter. Very gently push the pie into the pan until the top of the pie is even with the batter.

8 Pour on remaining batter to cover pie completely. Do not overfill the pan. If the pan is more than 3/4 full, you may have to use a turkey baster to remove some batter. Yes, there will be some leftover batter; bake it separately for a perfect midnight snack. Don't be surprised if the batter boils over a bit while cooking—it's bound to happen. Cut off the overflow with a serrated knife and eat it. It's delicious!

Bake Pie-Stuffed Cake Layers

one at a time at 350° for 45 to 50 minutes. Use the classic toothpick test to make sure the batter is thoroughly cooked. You don't want to underbake your Cherpumple and you don't want to overbake it. If your grandma is there, ask her if it's done; she'll know.

Cool,

then carefully remove pie-stuffed cakes from pans, cover with plastic wrap, and refrigerate until it's time to stack and frost.

Frosting Your Cherpumple

is the easy part. Stack and frost it on the sturdiest cake plate you can get your sticky fingers on, because it weighs a ton. Decorate your Cherpumple if you wish. I prefer to serve mine simply frosted. Remember the Cherpumple show is on the inside. Refrigerate until a couple of hours before you present and serve it.

Never crack. Even if your Cherpumple does.

SHOWTIME

Display Your Cherpumple

centered high on the most promi-nent table in the house. Spotlight it if you can. When it's high time to serve, gather your guests around your colossal pie-stuffed cake, and warn them about what they are soon to experience. To accentuate the wow factor of three pies stuffed into three cakes, the first piece you cut should be an entire quarter of the cake.

On the count of three, squeal like a pig as you push the knife down through all the layers as hard as you can. Slowly remove the massive chunk of

Cherpumple and plop it on a big plate. Be fully prepared for gasps and aahs as your guests experience the wonder of it for the first time. Be forewarned, one or more of your snootier guests may be horrified by the sight of it and may run away screaming. But trust me, they'll be back, begging for a big piece. We might as well get it out in the open: The Cherpumple is out of this world. It generates its own glow from within. It has super-powers far beyond the grasp of the universe we live in. Behold the glory of the almighty Cherpumple!

Cherpumple Dreams Do Come True!

I've spent far more time than I care to admit daydreaming that someday I'd get to ride in a parade, high atop a giant piece of Cherpumple. Then designers Kevin Kidney and Jody Daily and the float builders of the legendary Anaheim Halloween Parade surprised me by carefully crafting this great big, giant slice of hand-painted, plywood, pie-stuffed cake on wheels. The towering slice, oozing with cream cheese frosting, made its delicious debut by rolling through the streets of Disneyland's hometown in the 95th Annual Anaheim Halloween Parade. Seeing the throngs of smiling faces lining the streets, the cops all smiling, and civic pride at a fever pitch was as sweet as the Cherpumple itself.

Ready to roll!
Backstage at the Anaheim
Halloween Parade.

191

THANKYOULAND ★ I KNOW!

A super-duper extra-special thank you to collaborator, creative director, and designer extraordinaire Kathy Kikkert, who graciously and gleefully guided this book every step of the way, and without whom it never would have happened.

Thank you to Prospect Park publisher Colleen Dunn Bates for believing in this project, and also to her fine staff, Dorie Bailey, Caitlin Ek, and Katelyn Keating, as well as to publicist Trina Kaye.

Thank you to my terrific team: "Slibrarian" Teresa Kennedy, who diligently keeps track of my "slibrary" archive; ever-dapper manager Scott Marcus; always calm, cool, and collected Test Kitchen assistant Julie Richards; and bookkeeper Nancy Jacobs.

And for their contributions to this book, thank you to Collector Patrick Arlt, Sugar Egg Artist Ashley Augustine, Puppeteer Bob Baker, Hearse Owner Randy Bergum, Chef Matt Blansett, Synchronized Swimming Champion Molly Brown, Columbia Memorial Space Center Director Ben Dickow, Designer Jody Daly, Collector Lee Herendeen, Designer Kevin Kidney, Photographer Gary Krueger, Collector Jenny Kuller, Crafter Lisa Lazoff, Collector Janie Ellis, Production Assistant Kelly Martin, Restaurateur Monica May, Collector Denis Morella, Floating Christmas tree mastermind Jeff Neppl, Collector Judd Nissen, Ceramicist Mikel Parton, Ballusionist Brian Potvin, Jell-O Expert Michelle Quillas, Historian George Redfox, Float Builder Kelly Roberts, Collector Laurie Romanaggi, Candymakers Jerry and Suzy Rowley, Tech Wizard Stephen Schafer, Hallmark Historian Mark Spencer, Gingerbread-house Maker Oscar Streit, Chef Kristen Trattner, TV Personality Barry Weiss, and Designer Michael Uhlenkott. Most of all, thank you to my dear mother, Donna Givens, who taught me I could do anything in life I wanted!

Thank you to those who provided the following images:
Stefanie Augello (pages 8, 9)
David Eppen (page 14)
John Eng & Adrienne Biondo (page 124)
Heather David (page 31, upper right)
Fabian Fioto (page 3)
Edna Fitzgerald and Lloyd Laster (pages 138, 139)
Ric Griffith (page 68)
Kathy Kikkert (page 58 lower left, 100-105, 168-169)
Julie Klima (page 106)
Pam Madalone (page 48, upper left)
Nathan Pata (page 191)
Sean Teagarden (pages 142, 143)
Dora Wren (page 122 upper right)
ALL OTHER IMAGES IN THIS BOOK
ARE FROM THE CHARLES PHOENIX COLLECTION.

Charles Phoenix's suits tailored by Jonathan Behr of Los Angeles.
Deep Sea Dive shirt (page 100) by Sir Charles of Phoenix for Pinup Girl.

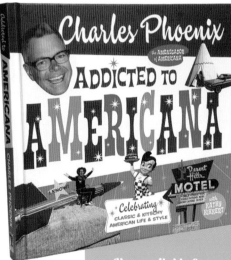

Charles Phoenix
the AMBASSADOR of AMERICANA
ADDICTED TO AMERICANA
Celebrating CLASSIC & KITSCHY AMERICAN LIFE & STYLE
with KATHY KIKKERT

Also available from Prospect Park Books!

PROSPECT PARK BOOKS

PUBLISHED BY PROSPECT PARK BOOKS
2359 Lincoln Ave.
Altadena, CA 91001
www.prospectparkbooks.com

Distributed by Consortium
www.cbsd.com

Library of Congress Cataloging in Publication Data is on file with the Library of Congress. The following is for reference only:

Names: Phoenix, Charles, author
Titles: Holiday Jubilee: Classic & Kitschy Festivities & Fun Party Recipes (2019)
Identifiers: ISBN 978-1-945551-35-2 (hardback)
Subjects: Pop culture; Crafts & Hobbies: Holiday & Seasonal; Cooking: Entertaining; Reference: Curiosities & Wonders

CREATIVE DIRECTION & DESIGN BY KATHY KIKKERT

Printed in China

CHARLES PHOENIX was born to celebrate classic and kitschy American life and style. He is a showman, food crafter, tour guide, and author of several books, including *Addicted to Americana*. Visit www.charlesphoenix.com for retro slide show performance dates, Test Kitchen videos, and lots more!

KATHY KIKKERT is a midcentury-obsessed creative director, graphic designer, vintage sign photographer, and type geek. She designed and collaborated with Charles on *Addicted to Americana*. Visit www.kikkertdesign.com for more fun retro modern design!